TOTAL TUNING FOR THE CLASSIC

MG MIDGET
A-H SPRITE

DANIEL STAPLETON

VELOCE PUBLISHING PLC
PUBLISHERS OF FINE AUTOMOTIVE BOOKS

Also published by Veloce is *Alfa Romeo Giulia GT & GTA Coupé* by John Tipler

First published in 1992 by -
Veloce Publishing Plc,
Godmanstone,
Dorset DT2 7AE,
England.

ISBN 1 874105 08 1
ISBN 1 874105 12 X (Paperback Edition)

Readers with ideas for automotive books, or books on other transport or related hobby sub-jects, are invited to write to the Editorial Director of Veloce Publishing at the above address.

British Library Cataloguing In Publication Data -
Stapleton, Daniel N. J.
        Total Performance Tuning: Classic MG Midget and Austin Healey Sprite
        I. Title
629. 28

Typesetting (in Avant Garde 10pt), design and page make-up all by Veloce on Apple Mac.

Printed and bound in the UK.

Cover photographs: Front, Dave Whyley's 1960 Sprite photographed by James Mann and cour-tesy of *Your Classic* magazine; Rear, Barry Coughlan's 1380cc Midget leads Rob Lea's 1360cc Midget in the Peter May Engineering/ Halfords Tools Modified Midget championship race at the MG Car Club's Silverstone meeting in May 1992, courtesy of Chris Harvey.

Publisher's note: the majority of line drawings and the small vignettes which are used for decoration are reproduced by courtesy of Unipart Interna-tional Ltd.

FOREWORD BY DAVID VIZARD

:44   07/07/95   :
TH CODE:085985
STOMER NOT PRESENT
ILL HOUSE BOOKS
STVILLE   BOSTON
443727.0013   540436157211814

ISA CREDIT
2982848483
96   KEYED

ANK YOU
7.99

. . . .

All too often practical books on performance tuning are written by those with little or no personal experience of actually doing the jobs described: when the reader tries to do the work, the writer's shortcomings soon become obvious!

Fortunately, Daniel Stapleton can put himself into the shoes of his readers so well that it seems as though he is turning the screwdrivers and pulling on the spanners and doing the very jobs he describes. His hands-on experience has taught him about the many small and unexpected problems and, of course, the real pitfalls that the reader - without such information - could easily fall foul of.

For all Sprite and Midget owners this book represents good solid "how to" step-by-step instructions, plus details of the results you are likely to get - all achievable with only what I would call a typical enthusiast's toolbox. If you have a Sprite or Midget and are relatively inexperienced at modifying for high performance, then I can almost guarantee that this book will pay for itself from the first significant job you tackle.

DAVID VIZARD
California

ACKNOWLEDGEMENTS

I would like to acknowledge the help, advice, encouragement, assistance and prayers of various people who helped me put this book together and without whom it would not have been possible -

Alan Abercrombie of Michelin Tyres plc, Julia Ashton of Corbeau Equipe Ltd, Simon Atherton, The Austin Healey Club, Roger Bishop of Serck Marston, Matt Brazier, Pete Bulman (Pastor of my Christian Fellowship and machinist!), Peter Baldwin of Marshall's of Cambridge, Norman Barker of AP Racing, Dan Boon of NGK Sparkplugs, Michael C. Brown - Photographer, Ray Chadlee of AP, John Chappel of Advanced Products (K & N Filters), Andy Chivers of R T Quaife Engineering Ltd, David Clarkson, Contract Distribution Services Ltd, John Cracknell of Serck Marston, Rae Davis of Motobuild, George Demitriou of Minor Mania, Keith Dodd of Mini Spares, Jonothan Douglas of Induction Technology Group Ltd, Eight Clubs Ltd, Chris Eyles of Weber Concessionaires, John Fenning of Stockbridge Racing (Willans), Jim Garvey, Sharon 'Goldilocks' Golding, Steve Green of Goodyear Tyres, Geoff Hale (Austin Healey Club Racer), Nick Hall of Safety Devices, Aaron Hammon of Victoria British Ltd, Dave Hardy of Hardy Engineering, Derek Hibbert of Sport Photography, Mike Hodder of Spax, Pete 'I slow down for Horses' Holden (Midget Racer), Peter Huxley of Fuel System Enterprise (FSE), Steve Jones - Photographer, Gail Latham of Serck Marston, Mark Lee of Lifeline, Simon A. Lee of Janspeed, Charles Leonard of Carcraft, Madeleine and Russell Lightning of Lightning Studios, Alan Ling of T.F. Bell & Co (Insurance Brokers) Ltd, Richard Longman, Peter May of Peter May Eng Ltd, The MG Owners Club, Mum, Peter McBride of Ron Hopkinson MG Parts Centre, Bob McIvor of Microdynamics, John P MacPhail of Reco Prop, Sharon Munro (Line Drawings), Davina Newsham of Unipart, Mike Nixon of Wellington Sea-life photography, Oselli Eng Ltd, George Owen of Goodridge, Simon Page (Austin Healey Racer), Tim Parsley of Marshall's of Cambridge, Joyce Pearce - Editor of *Revcounter*, John Peters of Sports & Classics, Robert Pocock of Kool Louvres, Andy Pringle of Castrol, Michael Quaife of R T Quaife Engineering Ltd, Steve Rae of Goodridge, Steve Renouf of Safety Devices, Dave Robinson (Line Drawings), Alan Rock of Stack Ltd, Paul 'Rodders' Rodman (1500 MG Midget racer), Philip A. Rogers - Photographer, Richard E Rooks, Steve Rollin of Northwest Import Parts, Fred Scatley Photography, Pat Smith of Safety Devices, Phil Stapleton (my brother), Rosemary Stapleton (my big sister), Simon 'Ex RAF' Sinclair, The Sprite and Midget Club, Tina Sweeney, Charlotte Thoday, Steve Tonks Engineering manager of Unipart International, David Vizard, Nick Warliker MIHORT, Simon 'Ex Army' Watson, Weber Concessionaires Ltd, Helena Wilkinson, David Williams of Stack Ltd.

INTRODUCTION

The background to this book is, of course, my own Mk4 Sprite (SOF 333H). I have owned this car for over seven years since I purchased it with the wings (fenders) held on by rope! This car, often to my Sister's and Mother's annoyance has swallowed more time and money than anyone other than a fellow enthusiast could imagine, yet it has been largely faithful and very reliable. I am proud of my own car and its capabilities even though close friends, after riding in the car, have often been uncomplimentary and sometimes rude about it ... and my driving! One friend, and mentioning no names (John Fenwick), is not an enthusiast and calls it "The Chariot", preferring to walk or cycle in preference to my giving him a lift.

In writing this book my main aim has been to include as many projects as possible that will be of interest and practical use to Sprite and Midget enthusiasts. Where the project is a modification carried out on my own car, it is explained in great depth to illustrate particular points and likely pitfalls. I believe the reader will find these explanations useful because, whilst some parts and component manufacturers supply fitting instructions, a great many do not or the instructions are only in brief note form. In many cases,

This was my car when I had had it only a few months and it was still relatively standard.

Top left: This is a shot of the engine in my car during my early ownership: most of the original tuning parts coming from my written-off 1300cc Mini. Gradually, I got the engine fully sorted out and producing reliable and decent horse-power.

Centre left: Although the view-point is different, you can easily see how much has changed under the bonnet of the car from when I first had it. Note the large Weber carb and what I consider to be a reasonably tidy engine compartment.

Bottom left: Another look at the engine in my car, this time from a different angle.

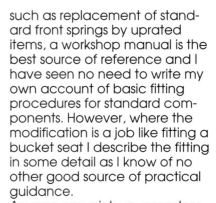

such as replacement of standard front springs by uprated items, a workshop manual is the best source of reference and I have seen no need to write my own account of basic fitting procedures for standard components. However, where the modification is a job like fitting a bucket seat I describe the fitting in some detail as I know of no other good source of practical guidance.

Anyone can pick up a random collection of performance parts and fit them to their car, but they will not necessarily end up with a satisfactory end product. I have found that some seemingly good tuning ideas do not always work as well in practice as was expected ... Some modifications are best done in conjunction with others or need some simple but vital finishing touch such as relief with a file. An instance would be fitting the Aldon anti tramp bars which need much minor modification if you already use, or plan to use, very wide tyres. The book covers all these hard-learned lessons to save you from the pitfalls I almost fell into and some that I did.

Some of the modifications

This was one of the last photos I took of the car before finishing the book and, since the engine and gearbox were out at the time, had to take the shot on the garage forecourt. By comparison with the original picture you will see a number of modifications, some very subtle.

described do not consist of ready-made kits or parts that you can just go out and buy but are my own simple and original ideas. One such modification is the two-speed wiper mod, from which sprang the first ever article I wrote and which led me on to other articles and, ultimately, this book. The two-speed wiper modification is not only one of the easiest to carry out but is extremely cheap and very, very useful: it has certainly given me endless satisfaction in the often wet British climate.

My intention is that the information and guidance in this book will have a wide range of usefulness, giving practical help to those with an almost standard car and those seeking a start in motorsport.

This book will show you what tuning options there are but choice of specification will have to be yours. For instance what I consider to be the ideal road or novice race suspension set-up another driver might find appalling or simply too ambitious for the road. Your choice, I hope, will be influenced by my own

experiences and the equipment options and compatibility I have been able to discover. It's likely, too, that your finances will only permit limited modifications and, where appropriate, I indicate those which are necessities and those which are desirable modifications. The book, I believe, has sufficient depth and usefulness to appeal to the home mechanic and a racing team.

The book does not contain an extensive engine tuning chapter. The reason for this is that I refer the reader to David Vizard's *Tuning BL's A -Series Engine*, the definitive work on tuning the Sprite/Midget A-series engine. This is simply the most authoritative book on the subject and like a workshop manual is more a necessity than an option if you are serious about getting to grips with your car. Yet, where I feel amplification on an engine related matter is worthwhile I do so. An example of this is the conversion to DCOE Weber carburation which, at face value, seems relatively simple, but final

choices on manifold and air filter can have far reaching consequences not least of which is trying to refit the bonnet!

To add interest and an incentive for the reader I have included some details on a couple of successful racing cars.

I hope that long suffering wives and girlfriends and possibly bank managers will draw some solace from the fact that modifying the Sprite/ Midget is very worthwhile and that the end product will beat a modern hot hatch absolutely hands down should that be your particular aim. My car may not be the best Sprite in the world but has given me enormous satisfaction and I have only ever attempted to attack it in a Basil Fawlty fashion once (that I can remember).

Never give up on your own project and should you ever have recourse to criticise this book, have information for inclusion in a future edition or wish to seek my advice, I will be only to happy to hear from you - via a letter to the publisher.

I hope you will both enjoy reading the book and recommend it to your friends.

Daniel Stapleton
Stowmarket, England

CONTENTS

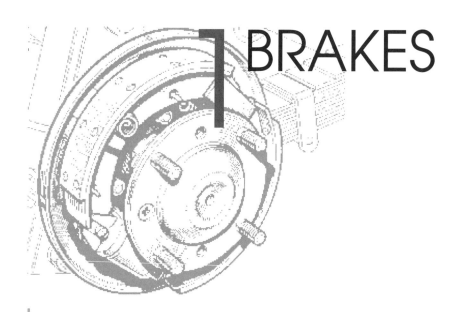

1 BRAKES

Introduction

With most improvements and modifications in this book being dedicated to achieving higher speed and acceleration I felt that the first priority should be a car with the capability to stop in a shorter distance. This chapter gives guidance on some approaches to improving your Sprite/Midget's brakes.

The brakes on the Sprite/Midget are quite good in standard form, assuming that the components are in sound condition and well maintained. One reason the standard brakes are effective is that the car is light in relation to the size of the brakes. I consider that the brakes are of sound condition when they meet the following criteria. Front discs need to be free of corrosion and scoring and of adequate thickness. As the discs get older they get thinner through being worn away and consequently have less capacity to absorb heat energy. Rear drums friction surfaces need to be similarly corrosion free and, like the discs, if they are well used they will be thinner, creating an added problem of lack of adjustment for the handbrake. Drum brakes must be properly adjusted. Both disc pad and brake shoe friction material must be uncontaminated and have plenty of life left. Brake fluid should also be less than two years old and kept that way by being changed regularly. It is vital that there are no leaks, cracks or corrosion affecting the brake pipes and check, of course, that calliper and drum wheel cylinder pistons are not seized (frozen) or corroded.

It is important to note that post-1977 Midgets have quite a few differences to early cars in the hydraulics as they have a dual line brake system so you will

Car use	Fluid spec	Metal braided hose	Friction material front/rear	Servo	Bias valve	Disc size
Std road	DOT 4	Yes	Standard	Opt	No	Std
Mild road	DOT 4	Yes	Standard	Opt	No	Std
Fast road or mild competition	DOT 4	Yes	Mintex M171/20	Yes	Opt	Std or large
All-out competition	AP550 /600	Yes	Ferodo DS11/ Mintex M20	Opt	Yes	Consider large discs

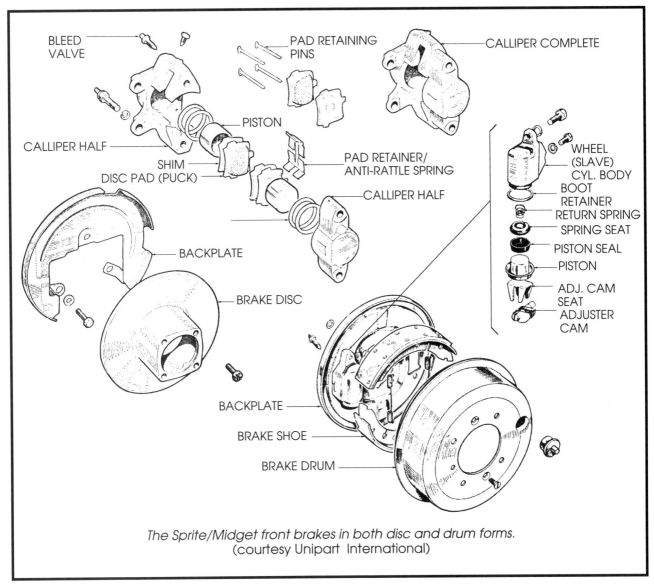

CALLIPER COMPLETE

BLEED VALVE

PAD RETAINING PINS

PISTON

CALLIPER HALF

SHIM

DISC PAD (PUCK)

PAD RETAINER/ ANTI-RATTLE SPRING

CALLIPER HALF

BACKPLATE

BRAKE DISC

WHEEL (SLAVE) CYL. BODY

BOOT

RETAINER

RETURN SPRING

SPRING SEAT

PISTON SEAL

PISTON

ADJ. CAM SEAT

ADJUSTER CAM

BACKPLATE

BRAKE SHOE

BRAKE DRUM

The Sprite/Midget front brakes in both disc and drum forms.
(courtesy Unipart International)

Modification options

The accompanying chart shows the modification options available and prioritizes them according to intended vehicle use.

Friction material

One of the first things you must consider is the brake friction material itself; *ie* the stuff on the disc pads and shoes. Standard brake friction material may not

need to be extra careful when modifying the system.

be able to cope with frequent and heavy braking applications, particularly if the car is faster than standard with the resultant effect of brake fade. What happens when the brakes fade is that the heat generated by braking is cooking the friction material until the resin in the material burns. Depending on how overheated the material and resin has become the damage may be temporary or permanent. The symptoms of brake fade are reduced braking efficiency, long brake pedal travel (caused by the brake fluid overheating) and a strong burning smell.
Having decided that a change

to a higher performance brake friction material is necessary for the car you now need to consider your precise needs. Precise because despite some advertising claims, brake pads are distinctly split into race braking material and other braking material. Though some braking material may be dual use by being suitable for mild competition applications and road use. Competition braking material is not dual use but will give unrivalled performance when used as intended.
My preferences are Ferodo DS11 material for pure competition applications and Mintex M171/M20 for dual application.

Use of too high a temperature range friction material will result in glazing of the pad surface and poor, if not dangerous, braking performance because such material simply will not work well at the temperatures generated by normal road use. Ferodo DS11 will give best performance between 500 - 650 degrees C (932 - 1202 degrees F). Mintex M171 has a working range of 50 to 500 degrees C (122 - 932 degrees F). To discover the temperature range your brakes are working within it is necessary to use Thermal paint on the brake discs and temperature indicator strips on the Brake calliper and drums, both available from suppliers like AP Racing. Full instructions are included in the kits and if used correctly their use will provide you with vital information on the temperature ranges the brakes are working within. A further point on brake temperatures is that it's necessary to get front and rear brakes operating within a fairly close temperature band otherwise you may end up with brake balance problems. Finally when you have selected suitable friction material be sure to follow the manufacturer's instructions on bedding it in before serious use!.

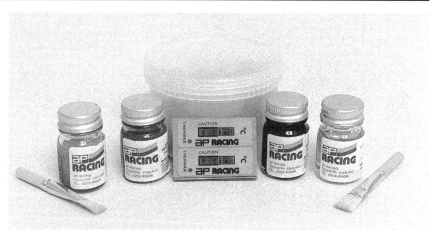

AP brake temperature recording kit.

Conventional brake and clutch fluids meet a DOT standard which relates to the 'dry' and wet boiling points of the fluid. DOT 4 is a higher temperature specification than DOT 3. The 'dry' standard is the important one because frequent change of fluid means the fluid never comes close to being classed as 'wet' (the 'wet' standard being a measurement of the fluid's boiling point after it has absorbed moisture). I recommend fluid changes every 12 months or less and monthly for race cars. I use Castrol fluid DOT 4 and have been very satisfied with it. However, if you have a pure racing application you might well look at the range of AP race fluids which have high

'dry' boiling points but need changing at more frequent intervals than those previously mentioned.

Drum to disc

The Sprite/Midget has a single circuit (not post-1977 cars), non-servoed disc/drum or (early cars) a drum/drum set up. The disc/drum set up will give the best results and it's possible to convert earlier cars to this specification by using the later car's components. You'll need wishbones, stub axles/uprights, discs, backplates and callipers together with the master cylinder from a later car to make the conversion following workshop manual instructions. New

Brake fluid

Your choice of brake fluid is also important to braking performance. There are two distinct types of brake fluid: Silicone and non Silicone. The principle difference between Silicone fluid and normal fluid is that the former is not hygroscopic (it does not absorb moisture from the atmosphere). Silicone-type brake fluid will preserve the interior of hydraulic pipes and will not affect seals at all it also has a long service life but is expensive and is not suitable for most competition applications.

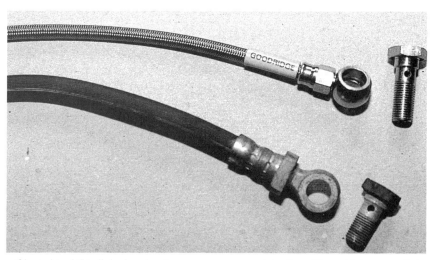

Standard flexible brake hose compared to the Goodridge metal braided equivalent.

hoses should be fitted.

Brake hoses

The first improvement is to get rid of the soggy pedal of the standard brakes. The fitting of Goodridge stainless steel brake hose will give the brakes a good solid feel. Goodridge no longer supply direct to the public but through a network of dealers (The dealer I have used for some time is Hobbsport).

Brake servo

The second big improvement is to fit a brake servo. A servo kit for the Sprite/Midget is fairly expensive, but it is money well spent. A servo kit should include the following parts: servo, mounting brackets, vacuum pipe and additional brake piping The AP kit (part No. LE 72696 pre-1977 cars) contains all these and a selection of fittings. The servo for the Sprite/Midget is different from most car brake servos in that it is separate from the master cylinder; for this reason it is known as a 'remote' type. The old Mini Cooper 'S' had a remote servo and the servo in most kits is the same type and size. Anything bigger than this is too large. Mini Spares of London can supply the servo and most of the parts, and from personal experience I have

AP brake servo kit complete ready to fit to a Sprite or Midget.

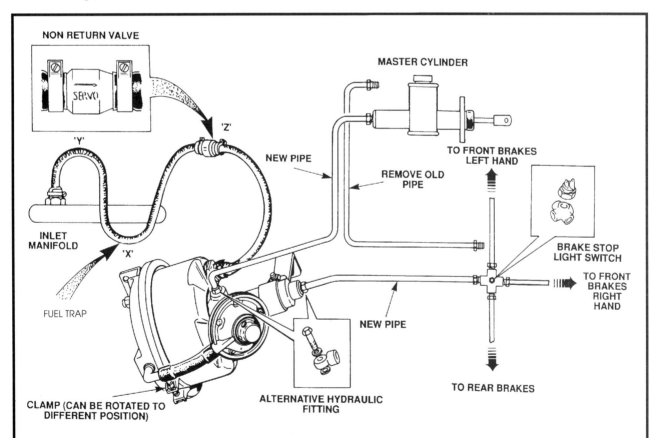

The AP brake servo kit is easy to fit and this drawing illustrates how the hydraulic piping is modified to put the servo in series between master cylinder and union. On my own installation I have not bothered with a non-return valve or fuel trap in the vacuum hose which has not caused me any grief (courtesy AP & redrawn by Dave Robinson/Sharon Monroe)

found them an excellent company to deal with, as are AP the manufacturers of the kit.

A servo works by using vacuum from the inlet manifold affecting one side of a large diaphragm to boost the hydraulic pressure. This in itself does not improve the car's braking capability but it does reduce the pedal pressure needed to be exerted by your right foot. This extra pressure from the servo allows full utilization of the car's braking potential as maximum braking is achieved at the point just before wheel lock-up. Of course, if you're a budding Mr/ Ms Universe don't bother with this mod; however, since most of us don't fit into that category then, as tyre width or gripping properties are increased, (ie use of slick tyres), it will become even more difficult to achieve a near lock-up condition at any given speed without a servo. An interesting point is that extremely few race car drivers use servo assisted brakes as they prefer a solid pedal, the servo inevitably adding some sponginess to the feel of the brakes.

A servo fitting kit should contain full fitting instructions but in case it doesn't, and for the benefit of readers who buy the components separately, I will detail fitting for you.

Fit the servo unit first. You can purchase brackets or fabricate your own from mild steel or aluminium sheet metal or strip. On a right-hand drive car the best place to fit the servo is just below the wiper motor with the narrow end pointing away from the front of the car. Left-hand cars may need a different location, the main objective is to try and keep all the brake and vacuum lines as short as possible. And, wherever you site the servo be sure you allow enough room for the bonnet to close ...

With the servo unit secured in place, next fit the vacuum pipe from the unit to the inlet manifold. Hobbsport can supply

Goodridge stainless braided hose and associated fittings suitable for servo/manifold vacuum pipe as well as cheaper rubber hose. The braided hose is desirable because it is much less likely to chafe and leak. If a leak developed in the vacuum hose the subsequent weakening of the fuel mixture might well be sufficient to cause detonation and could ultimately lead to engine (piston) failure. It's worth ensuring that your kit has the non-return valve type manifold union which allows a vacuum to be stored for longer periods of non-operation.

Most SU manifolds, standard or competition, will have provision for a servo vacuum pipe take-off and will only require the blanking bolt's removal and substitution by a hose union. Weber manifolds may not have this provision so the manifold will require removal - otherwise swarf will be sucked into the engine - for drilling and tapping. The last job will be fitting the hydraulic piping. The existing rigid piping from the brake master cylinder to the 4 way brake union is removed and

discarded. A new rigid pipe is run from the master cylinder to the servo hydraulic inlet. Note that all servos have an inlet and

Goodridge braided metal hose for servo vacuum take-off on Weber type manifold.

The servo unit should be positioned under the wiper motor. This side view (now with braided metal hose) illustrates the small bonnet (hood) clearance.

outlet, be sure you fit them the correct way round. Another new rigid pipe is used to run from the servo outlet to the 4 way union. When you purchase your pipe ask for the copper type: it's minimal extra expense but much greater corrosion resistance makes copper a preferable choice. If you wish, you can buy a brake pipe flaring kit yourself and make all your own pipes.

The braking system will require bleeding before use. Keep a close eye on the fluid level when bleeding as you have a lot of new pipe to fill with fluid. The quickest way to get air out of the system is by bleeding the servo outlet pipe just before it's screwed into the 4 way union and then connect it and bleed the rest of the system in the normal manner. A final note on bleeding is that some of those self-bleed gadgets rely on the threaded portion of the bleed nipple to prevent air being drawn into the hydraulic system. Thus, with the self-bleed gadget it's possible to draw air in on the return stroke of the pumping operation. It will only be a small amount, but if a job's worth doing it's worth doing right. Thanks to Paul Hobbs for that point - I never have trusted them but didn't have a good reason until Paul passed that tip on.

Brake bias valve

With the servo fitted and working it will now be much easier to achieve maximum braking capability, that is unless you now get premature rear wheel lock-up. Because of the Sprite/Midget's light back end and the weight transfer to the front during braking, the rear wheels tend to lock first and can start a tail slide. To eliminate this tendency it is necessary to fit an adjustable pressure limiting valve. The valve can be set or adjusted to restrict pressure to

the rear wheels as desired. The bias valve I use is the Lockheed item which is available from Ripspeed Ltd. There are other more expensive types available which give pre set selector positions and this type is available from Hobbsport.

To fit such a valve, disconnect the three brake pipes from the 3-way union which is mounted on the differential (axle) housing. Remove the union and replace with the bias valve. The brake line from the front of the car can be fitted to the valve.

The pipes which connect the 3-way union (new bias valve) to the rear drums have to be completely removed so that they can be re-flared to fit the bias valve unions. The type of flair that is required for the Lockheed valve is concave. Once the valve is in place and the pipes have been refitted, the system is bled in the usual manner. The brake balance from front to rear is controlled by winding in or out a small 'T' key in the valve itself.

An alternative but more expen-

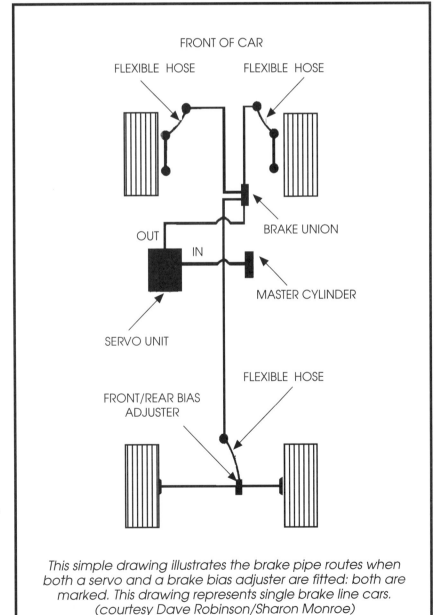

This simple drawing illustrates the brake pipe routes when both a servo and a brake bias adjuster are fitted: both are marked. This drawing represents single brake line cars. (courtesy Dave Robinson/Sharon Monroe)

sive solution to achieving brake balance would be to fit a dual master cylinder and use a brake balance bar. Unless you are building a race car I think that the extra expense and complexity means that this is a job for the experienced mechanic only.

Right: Large size discs as fitted to Simon Page's turbocharged frogeye. Note the additional top suspension link (effectively creating a wishbone) on this heavily modified car. The threaded rose-joints also allow total adjustability for optimum performance.

Below: Brembo discs have been recommended to me and are available specifically for the Sprite/Midget: these are vented items. (courtesy Contract Distribution Services Ltd/Patricia Newbold Photography)

Brake discs

Non-standard brake discs such as the Brembo items (available from Peter May Eng Ltd) produce superior braking performance. The Brembo part numbers are Sprite/Midget 08.1509.10 (steel wheels) and 08.1633.10 (wire wheels). A piece of late news just as this book was nearing completion is that the Sprite and Midget Centre now retail a large disc conversion kit which I have so far not had chance to evaluate. Though I have seen many race cars successfully using the Peter May Eng. large disc conversion. Opinion appears to be divided as to whether the large discs are really necessary even for racers ,so much more than that I cannot say. No one I know uses discs on the rear wheels of a road car and I certainly don't consider it necessary to fit them though (Morris) Minor Mania do retail a suitable kit.

Conclusion

Having finished uprating the brakes the result will speak for itself. You may ,however, wish to take your car to a local garage or brake centre and get them to do a full brake check on the rolling brake test machine. If you have completed the work competently then ,like me, you will find that your car's braking performance will far exceed the specified performance of the standard Sprite/Midget.

2 FRONT SUSPENSION

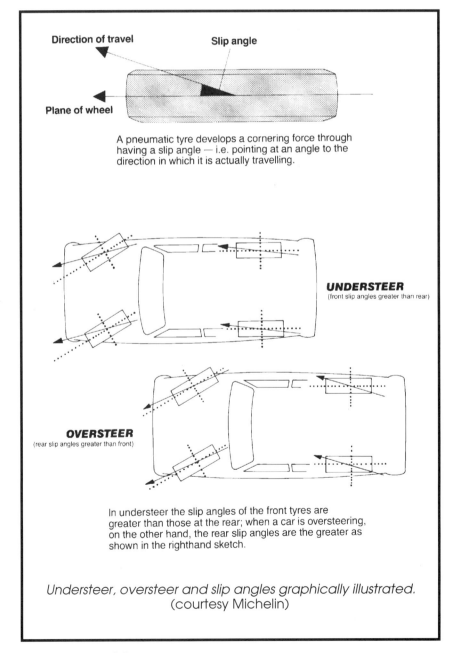

Direction of travel

Slip angle

Plane of wheel

A pneumatic tyre develops a cornering force through having a slip angle — i.e. pointing at an angle to the direction in which it is actually travelling.

UNDERSTEER
(front slip angles greater than rear)

OVERSTEER
(rear slip angles greater than front)

In understeer the slip angles of the front tyres are greater than those at the rear; when a car is oversteering, on the other hand, the rear slip angles are the greater as shown in the righthand sketch.

Understeer, oversteer and slip angles graphically illustrated.
(courtesy Michelin)

Introduction

Before modifying your car's front suspension decide how much you can afford to spend. Think, too, about what you want from the suspension: is it for fast road or motorsport use, or a compromise between the two? Also, it's most important to match rear suspension modifications to those applied at the front; for instance, a full race front end with a standard rear will not produce good results. The final point to consider is that it is, in my opinion, wise to modify the suspension a stage at time and thereby experience what affect each change produces. This will help you to tailor your car's handling characteristics to your own preference.

In case you are unfamiliar with the terms "understeer" and "oversteer" I will provide a brief explanation. Whenever a car turns, its tyres create a sideways or cornering force. This results in the tyre running with a "slip angle" (the angle between the direction in which it is pointing and the direction in which it is being forced to travel by the inertia of the car to which it is attached). The front and rear tyres rarely run at the same angle when the car is cornering. When the front tyres run the greatest slip angle the effect is known as "understeer" and is usually felt by the driver as the front end of the car wanting to run slightly wide of the cornering line. If the rear slip angle is the greater, the condition is known as "oversteer". The driver usually feels the rear end of the car wanting to run slightly wide of the corner. The Sprite/Midget is generally an oversteering car due to its rear drive layout. Careful selection of suspension parts and tyre width can ,however, change the standard characteristics of the car.

If your car's suspension is worn it's unlikely to give good results no matter how you set it up.

Therefore, ensure that all the suspension components are in very good order and, as with any tuning, remember the most effective way to modify is by replacing standard parts with performance parts in stages. Standard overhaul of the front suspension is described in workshop manuals. Another useful source of information is the Ron Hopkinson Spridget catalogue which has a well written "Hints and Tips" guide to suspension rebuilds.

Modification options

Here is a simple chart to give at least a few guidelines on how to make a good choice of matching front suspension components.

car doesn't have an anti-roll bar currently, when you do get around to purchasing and fitting one you'll not need to do any drilling, saving of both time and possible trouble. Ron Hopkinson offer a service where new or reconditioned wishbones can have a second grease nipple brazed in, which improves the lubrication of the fulcrum pin.

Bushes

When rebuilding your suspension you may wish to consider replacing all the standard compliant rubber bushes with bushes made in Nylatron or Bronze. These types of bushes will produce a much stiffer and tauter feel to the suspension.

Intended usage	Spring rate	Spring free length	Roll bar diameter	Shock absorber (damper) stiffness
Std/mild road use	271lbf/in (3.122kgf/m)	9.4/9.59/9.85in (238/244/250mm)	1/2 (12.7mm)	Std
Road use	280lbf/in (3.226kgf/m)	9.85in (250mm)	9/16 (14.2mm)	Std
	320lbf/in (3.686 kgf/m)	8.27in (210mm)	5/8 (15.8mm)	+ 30%
Fast road use	340lbf/in (3.917 kgf/m)	8.74in (222mm)	5/8 / 11/16 (15.8/17.4mm)	+ 30 to 50%
Comp. use	360lbf/in (4.147kgf/m)	8.03in (204mm)	11/16 or 3/4 (17.4mm or 19mm)	+ 50%
	400lbf/in (4.608kgf/m)	7.28in (185mm)	11/16 or 3/4 (17.4mm or 19mm)	as required
	430lbf/in (4.954kgf/m)	7.32in (186mm)	11/16 or 3/4 (17.4mm or 19mm)	as required

New wishbones

If your car's suspension wishbones need renewal always ask for replacement components with anti-roll bar holes pre-drilled whether your purchase is new or reconditioned wishbones. The reason for this is that even if your

However, the downside is that you might find the reduced compliance increases noise, vibration and harshness (NVH) to an unacceptable level for day-to-day use. Your circumstances and the other modifications you have made to the suspension will dictate whether you take this option or not.

Likewise it is possible to replace the anti-roll bar link with a metal rose jointed item.

Springs, stiffness and ride height

One of the key choices to make when choosing your car's

Above: Nylatron suspension bush sets.

Left: Rose-jointed adjustable anti-roll bar link on Simon Page's turbocharged Frogeye Sprite.

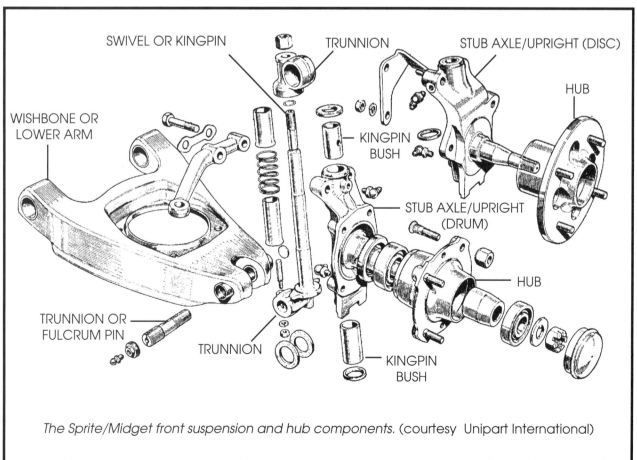

SWIVEL OR KINGPIN   TRUNNION   STUB AXLE/UPRIGHT (DISC)

HUB

WISHBONE OR LOWER ARM

KINGPIN BUSH

STUB AXLE/UPRIGHT (DRUM)

HUB

TRUNNION OR FULCRUM PIN

TRUNNION

KINGPIN BUSH

The Sprite/Midget front suspension and hub components. (courtesy Unipart International)

ride characteristics are the road springs themselves. Road springs govern ride stiffness to a large extent and also dictate ride height. Your choice of road spring will be based on the ride height you are looking for and how stiff you can go for your desired application. For instance, the smoother your intended road or track surface the lower and harder you can go if you choose. Several retail outlets and manufacturers will sell you road or fast road springs in a couple of different heights. Quite often these same people don't really know what they are selling you or what results you will get. I was once sold a set of lowered and very stiff springs for my Sprite: not only were they stiffer than nearly every racing Sprite's but lower too! Yet, I still found I got on quite well with them although I should have checked first to see what I was buying and, more importantly ,how they compared with the standard items.

As a simple guide, hard springs will give improved cornering and straight line stability. Reduced height springs will decrease body roll, lower the car's centre of gravity and reduce ground clearance.

The spring rate for all models is 271 lbf/in (3.127kgf/m) but there are three different standard spring heights as detailed in the table earlier in this chapter When you see a spring advertised as one inch lower ask yourself; one inch lower than which of the three standard heights? Ask the retailer what the exact measured height is. I would caution against a ride height reduced by much more than one inch (25.4mm) for any model except 1500 Midgets where an extra half inch (12.7mm) lower is acceptable, if the car is to be used on the public highway.

Some spring retailers appear unable to quote the spring poundages/rates or heights. Aftermarket spring poundages/

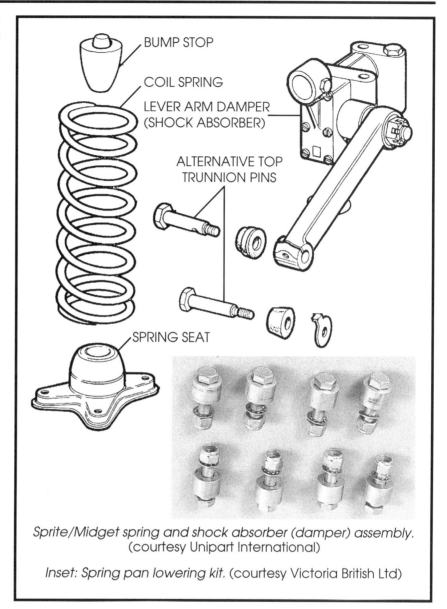

Sprite/Midget spring and shock absorber (damper) assembly. (courtesy Unipart International)

Inset: Spring pan lowering kit. (courtesy Victoria British Ltd)

rates for the Sprite/Midget are usually less than 450lbf/in (5.184 kgf/m) and springs taller in free length than 7.28 inches (185mm). My experience has been that you can get good advice on spring selection from Peter May Eng. Ltd who can also make to order any spring specification you request as can Motobuild. As a starting point and for road use I suggest springs that are one inch lower than standard and rated at around 320 lbf/in (3.687 kgf/m). For motorsport try lower and harder. Be careful how low you go and check (even with one inch lower springs) that there is

enough ground clearance for the exhaust system as this is generally the lowest point on the car. You may wish to rehang the system in a different fashion and I refer you to the chapter dealing with exhaust systems.

A change of spring is not the only way to lower the suspension. Although I have not tried them personally I do know that Motobuild Ltd and, in the USA, Victoria British Ltd, retail a spring pan lowering kit which lowers the spring in relation to the wishbone and this method can be used to lower the car in relation to any height of spring.

This method gives a much reduced ride height without the usually associated stiffness of shorter competition springs.

Camber and trunnions

Lowering of the front suspension changes the wheel camber: camber being the angle of the wheel's inward or outward lean in relation to the road surface. Correct camber angle can be restored by replacement of the rubber trunnion bushes with offset bronze bushes. Offset trunnion bushes allow camber adjustment as the centre hole is eccentric. Under hard cornering conditions the outside loaded wheel should be as near vertical in relation to the road or track surface as possible and this is the objective of camber adjustment. It may be an advantage to use the offset trunnion bushes even if you have not lowered your car's front suspension. However, it is possible to have too much of a good thing, and too much negative camber can reduce cornering efficiency and introduce a great deal of oversteer. I do not recommend negative camber for road cars and the ideal degree of negative camber for a racer will be a matter of personal choice after trial and error experiments.
Aldon Automotive Ltd make heat treated cast alloy trunnions that produce negative camber

Shock absorbers

Having looked at the springs, ride height and suspension stiffness the other major component is the shock absorber or damper - I prefer the term "damper" as it is a much more accurate description of what this piece of hardware actually does. On the Sprite/Midget the standard damper also acts as the top suspension wishbone/link. Like any damper its job is to stop spring oscillation (the Yo-Yo effect). Worn dampers will make the car pitch and roll through a corner. Change the springs and dampers at the same time and well before both are totally worn out. It's important to match spring and damper characteristics. A stiff spring on a soft damper will make the spring work very hard and wear out prematurely and the soft damper will not control the spring effectively. Similarly, a soft spring on a hard damper will leave the damper to do some of the spring's work and again cause premature wear. Dampers also have a pronounced affect on braking distance if worn or too soft. My experience of dampers is purely limited to road use and race applications will be very different to road solutions. Once you have made your spring selections, and assuming you are still using the lever arm unit, you will need to experiment with different internal valves in order to obtain a balance you are happy with. It is, of course, much easier to get a satisfactory result if you are using externally adjustable dampers.
When modifying the suspension on the Sprite/Midget the choice used to be uprated lever arm units or a telescopic conversion. I use the past tense here as Ron Hopkinson have now bought out Spridgebits and are not going to continue manufacturing the Spridgebits kit which had certain drawbacks. However, when this book was first produced the Ron Hopkins company was on the verge of launching a full handling kit for the Sprite/Midget.

Telescopic shock absorber conversion

Despite the drawbacks of the old telescopic shock absorber/damper conversion by Spridgebits it does have the one great advantage of utilising on-car adjustable telescopic dampers which are of real benefit to the racer but possibly of less interest to the road user. The Spridgebits conversion is quite simple, but when I bought mine there were no fitting instructions so I shall include details here. The kit retains the standard lever arm damper unit minus the valve, effectively leaving the lever arm unit to perform the role of a top link only. A large bracket is bolted on top of the lever arm unit using the existing bolts and fits against the inside of the inner wing (fender). This bracket is the mounting for a small U-shaped bracket which bolts onto the outboard side of the inner wing after drilling a hole through the inner wing to correspond with the one pre-drilled in the large bracket. Be sure the U-shaped bracket is tight and check periodically for slackening of its retaining bolt. Although not essential, I strongly recommend that you have a small, top mounting reinforcing plate welded onto the inner or outer surface of the inner wing or, best of all, both. This will prevent elongation of the bolt hole which is one of the drawbacks of the kit.
To locate the bottom eye of the telescopic damper a small bracket is bolted onto the rear flange of the wishbone. If your car's wishbone has the anti-roll bar holes (duplicated on both front and back flange of the wishbone) it is the rear set of holes that this bracket bolts to. If the wishbone doesn't have the holes you will need to drill them or replace the wishbone with a later item. The other main drawback of the kit will manifest itself here as, in time, the wishbone will crack around this lower mounting if a small reinforcement plate is not welded on .Once both top and bottom mountings are fixed the damper fastens to the top and bottom brackets. The tel-

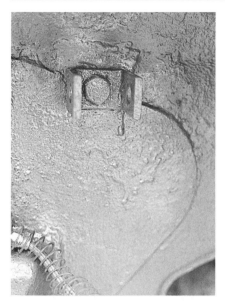

Far left: The U-bracket for the shock absorber top mounting on the Spridgebits telescopic conversion kit.

Left: The bottom shock absorber link for the Spridgebits kit is mounted on the side flange of the lower wishbone.

Below left: The Spridgebits telescopic conversion kit fitted. Note braided metal brake hose with additional protective 'spring'.

escopic damper can be of the on-car adjustable type which I feel is the beauty of the system. Also, as the damper is independent of the top suspension link, the the unit has a longer life than a lever-arm typedamper unit.

Should you obtain one of these kits and the shock absorbers wear out then replacement shock absorbers will be available from Spax Ltd, who supplied the originals, but quote the number of the old component which is usually found at the base of the unit.

A last point on the telescopic damper conversion is that it may cause the brake hose to rub against the road wheel when the wheel is on full lock. For this reason all kits were supplied with Goodridge steel braided hose but even so it is advisable to check the hose regularly for damage.

Anti-roll bar

Having covered dampers or, if you prefer, shock absorbers, it is important to look at what I consider is one of the greatest areas for improvement in Sprite/ Midget handling: fitting an uprated anti-roll bar and mountings. My experience has been that the biggest contribution to handling improvements come from the anti-roll bar. The bar reduces body roll or sway

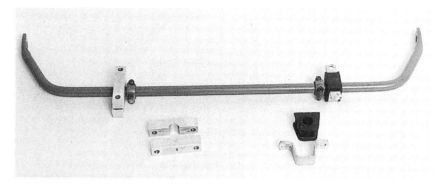

Above: Conventional non-adjustable anti-roll bar connecting link.

Top left: An anti-roll bar with both types of mounting block.

Centre left: Motobuild solid aluminium mounting block but fitted with hex-head rather than Allen bolts.

Left: Wishbone with anti-roll bar link and Spridgebits bottom link and shock absorber. The spring seat, which can be adjusted in height, can be clearly seen. Note that whilst the wishbone is removed the opportunity has been taken to renew all bushings - this is the right way to go about chassis tuning.

and for this reason is sometimes known as a 'sway bar'.
There are currently four different thickness of aftermarket anti-roll bar available for the Sprite/Midget, as detailed in the table earlier in this chapter. The thicker the bar the stiffer and harder the ride will be and the less the car will roll.
The standard anti-roll bar is mounted on rubber blocks bolted to the chassis legs. An alternative to these rubber blocks is solid aluminium blocks which stiffen up the ride even further. The aluminium blocks are direct replacements for the rubber blocks and the principle

An adjustable tie rod has been added to the damper arm/top link of this racing Spridget. The tie rod triangulates the damper arm and, effectively, turns it into a wishbone.

difference, apart from the obvious, is that they are secured by long Allen bolts rather than hexagon-headed bolts. In addition they have a grease nipple, the head of which invariably breaks off!

Motobuild retail aluminium wishbone mounting plates for anti-roll bars which have a weight advantage. It's also possible to rose joint the linkage from the mounting plate to the roll bar for added stiffness as previously mentioned.

On my road car I've always used the 11/16inch (17.4mm) anti-roll bar in conjunction with the Motobuild solid mounting blocks with no problems and I find the ride very satisfactory, although most of my passengers complain vehemently!

Fitting of any anti-roll bar is straightforward and I suggest you check the workshop manual for precise details. Note that although some very early cars are not fitted with an anti-roll bar, the chassis mountings will be in place and the fitting of later wishbones will allow the fitting of an anti-roll bar.

Conclusion

This chapter has detailed my experience with the Sprite/ Midget's front suspension but this is a vast subject and one with many variables. Ultimately, the suspension set-up for your car will be dictated not only by what you can afford and your intended application but, perhaps most importantly, your own driving preferences.

It's also true to say that unless you are a serious motor racing contender searching for 10/ 10ths performance, you'll find it relatively easy to improve your Sprite/Midget's handling to a substantial degree.

3 REAR SUSPENSION

Introduction

The Sprite/Midget rear suspension is straightforward in design. It consists of a live axle, leaf springs and lever arm dampers (shock absorbers). Early Sprites/Midgets have quarter-elliptic leaf springs while later models use half-elliptic. The 1500cc Midget has 6 leaves to its springs as opposed to 5 leaves on the other half-elliptic cars.

If you find that your car handles badly it is not due to poor design as, when in good condition, the standard system is fine for cars with standard performance; more likely the suspension is simply worn out after many years of service. The most cost effective way to modify the rear suspension is to replace standard parts with modified ones during a suspension rebuild. When working on the Sprite/Midget's rear suspension I recommend that the best and safest way to tackle a rebuild or fitment of modified parts is to support the car with proper axle stands (jack stands) placed just forward of the front spring hangers. Also, be sure to chock the front wheels. The suspension can be worked on a side at a time or both sides simultaneously but my experience has been that it is far better to work on only one side at a time especially if fitting the telescopic damper conversion

Modification options

To help you decide what is best for your car here is another

Intended usage	Nylatron bushing	Telescopic dampers	Red. ride height	Anti-tramp bars
Std mild road	No	Recommended	No	No
Fast road	Optional	Recommended	1 inch (2.54mm)	Yes (if over 85bhp at rear wheels)
Comp. use	Yes	Recommended	2 inches (5.08cm)	Yes

Left: Simon Page's fabricated rear suspension with vertical shock absorbers: here supported on an axle stand.

Centre left: Motobuild Nylatron bushes for rear springs.

Telescopic shock absorbers (dampers) conversion

If you discover your rear dampers are ineffective or not suitable for fast driving you may replace them with uprated items. However, rather than fit uprated lever arm dampers I recommend an alternative. Spax shock absorbers manufacture a kit which replaces the Armstrong lever arm shocks with adjustable telescopic dampers (shock absorbers). Not only is the conversion neat and simple it provides for dampers that are on-car adjustable. Fitting is straightforward as I will detail, although the Spax kit does contain some fitting instructions. It is possible to get a telescopic shock-absorber conversion for quarter-elliptic sprung cars but as I've not encountered such an installation yet, I can't really comment on likely fitting problems nor on the efficacy of the modification. The Spax kit does contain fitting instructions and a diagram.

With the old Armstong unit removed the first task is to fit the Spax mounting bracket for the telescopic damper. This bracket is very strong and is fitted to the car where previously the lever arm unit was located. The bracket uses the existing holes so no drilling is necessary. The link arm is discarded altogether. The link arm bracket is swopped with an opposite handed bracket. You may use the bracket from the other side of the car or purchase a new one (if necessity dictates your having to work on one side of the

simple chart which is a guide to modifying your car's rear suspension.

Nylatron bushes

Before purchasing replacement rubber bushes including the ones between the springs and plates and for the all the suspension pick-ups on your car, consider the use of a Nylatron bushes. This type of bush offers greater resistance to movement in the suspension and will give a tauter feel. The Nylatron bushes will, unfortunately, also give a

harder ride as they transmit more shock than a rubber bush. The change to Nylatron from rubber is more of a competition modification than a road one. However, you may feel the negative aspect is negligible, or worth living with and fit Nylatron bushes to a road car. The bushes are available from Motobuild Ltd. Fitting should be straightforward but the bushes may need a little fettling with a file or rasp to get them to fit, do not force them. To further aid fitting lubricate the bushes with Copperslip or a similar copper-based grease

The fitting diagram for the Spax conversion kit for telescopic rear shock absorbers.
a) Upper bracket. b) Bottom mounting bracket against spring.
c) Shock absorber. d) Rear axle. e) Front of vehicle. f) Top bracket securing bolts using existing holes. g) Bottom securing bolt for shock absorber. (courtesy Spax, redrawn by Sharon Monroe)

Rear springs and lowering blocks

I have found Motobuild a good company from which to purchase uprated rear springs and Rae Davis can offer excellent advice on the best springs for your particular car. You can buy leaf springs in a variety of ride heights and stiffnesses for both quarter and half-elliptic sprung cars. Some springs are uprated by the use of extra leaves but it is not so much how many leaves but rather the lengths of the top leaves that stiffens the suspension. Of course, race cars which have been substantially lightened may not need stiffer springs at all and, generally speaking, Sprites and Midgets do not require stiffer rear springs. Before buying new springs have a think about the ride height of the car. If you lower the ride height then the centre of gravity is also lowered: this will reduce body roll and increase stability. Motobuild sell reduced

Above: Spax telescopic conversion kit for Sprites and Midgets with half-elliptic rear springs (the majority).

suspension at a time). The link arm bracket is then refitted, upside down but otherwise in the original manner.
The Spax telescopic damper will locate on the bracket fitted to the car at its top end, and to

the lever arm bracket at its bottom end. Before you connect the damper)shock absorber) you will of course need to fit the spring if you removed it for other suspension work.
The Spax units are on-car adjustable: my advice is to start at the hardest setting and work down to softer settings until you are content with the way the car handles.

Above: Spax telescopic shock absorber conversion kit fitted - note bottom shock absorber mounting and anti-tramp bar.

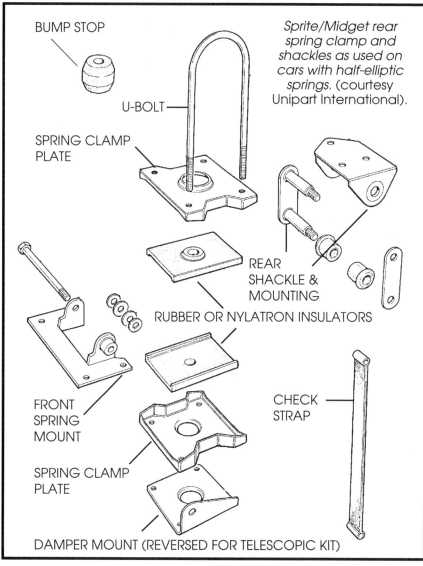

BUMP STOP

U-BOLT

SPRING CLAMP
PLATE

Sprite/Midget rear spring clamp and shackles as used on cars with half-elliptic springs. (courtesy Unipart International).

REAR
SHACKLE &
MOUNTING

RUBBER OR NYLATRON INSULATORS

FRONT
SPRING
MOUNT

SPRING CLAMP
PLATE

CHECK
STRAP

DAMPER MOUNT (REVERSED FOR TELESCOPIC KIT)

ride height springs, though I prefer an alternative method or a combination of two methods. Aside from buying reduced height springs to lower the ride height you can use a lowering block. The block effectively raises the axle in relation to the spring, thereby achieving the same thing as would a reduced ride height spring.

The lowering block is made in aluminium and is inserted between the axle and the spring. The car's intended use will dictate the height reduction you choose (see option chart at start of chapter) but whatever your choice make sure it matches the reduction in ride height at the front of the car. Blocks come in the following sizes: one inch (25.4mm), one and a half inches (38.1mm) and two inches (50.8mm). Extra long U-bolts for use with the blocks are normally included when buying lowering blocks if you buy the blocks separately you will need to source them from your local accessory shop. Kits are available from Motobuild Ltd and some other Sprite and MG specialists.

Fitting is as follows: first support the car with suitable axle stands. Support the axle separately, preferably by use of a trolley or bottle jack. Next unbolt the existing U-bolts and remove them. You can now lower the axle until it drops sufficiently to allow insertion of the block. Once the block is inserted refasten the spring to the axle using the extra long U bolts.

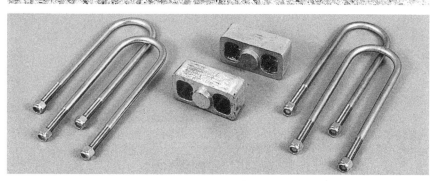

Left centre: Rear leaf spring, lowering block and Aldon anti-tramp bar as used on my own car to good effect. Take the opportunity to fit new spring eye-bushes and, if necessary, new shackle pins too.

Left: Rear spring lowering blocks and U-bolts. (courtesy Victoria British Ltd).

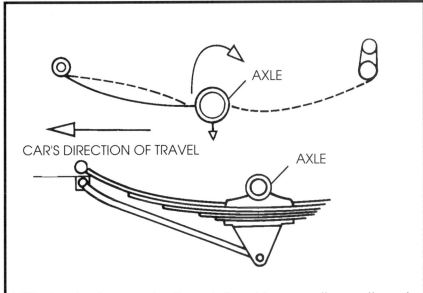

With standard suspension the rotational forces acting on the axle can twist or 'wind up' the spring, causing axle tramp. This is prevented by the anti-tramp bar which restricts axle movement to rising and falling. (drawn by Dave Robinson/Sharon Munro)

bracket is bolted to the car's underbody below the front spring hanger plate using the existing holes but slightly longer bolts, while the rear bracket .is fixed to the U-bolt clamp by passing the U-bolts through the bracket and re-tightening them. I have found it necessary to fettle front and rear brackets slightly to get a good fit. The principle area that needs attention will be the edges that sit over spring, as it may impinge on the rivet of the spring clamp, it is easily ground or filed away to give clearance.

If you use the anti-tramp bars with the Spax telescopic conversion it may be necessary to grind the rear anti-tramp

Below: The rear mounting for the anti-tramp bar.

Anti-tramp bars and Panhard rod

For most drivers the previously described modifications will provide all the improvement required. However, for cars putting out over 85bhp at the rear wheels and being used competitively, or simply very enthusiastically, there are a couple more worthwhile modifications that can be made. When a car is accelerated hard from a standstill the wheels can twist the axle and wind up the spring until the spring rebounds: the sequence then repeats itself. This is known as "axle-tramp" and can be seen when the driven wheels hop up and down during acceleration. Axle-tramp is not only detrimental to good acceleration but can also break the differential casing. The total solution is to fit Aldon Automotive anti-tramp bars although, if the condition is not too bad, then a Nylatron bush kit can help alleviate the problem.

The anti-tramp bar is fitted between two brackets; the front

mounting bracket. This is done to give clearance between the bracket and the link arm bracket. Also, I recommend the centre hole on the base of the rear anti-tramp bracket be extended to the bar pick-ups by drilling through them. Check bracket to tyre clearance and file centre bracket if necesary. Aldon Automotive can also supply a Panhard rod kit for the Sprite/Midget as can Peter May Eng. The Panhard rods are there to provide sideways location for the axle. The kit is specific to either Armstrong shocks or telescopic conversion so specify which you are using when you place your order. If you are using very wide wheels I would recommend this kit.

Anti-roll bar

One item discovered just in time to be included in the book is the availability of rear anti-roll bars for the Sprite/Midget. These items appear only to be sold in the USA and in theory they

should work fine. Naturally, I would be most interested to hear from readers who have experience of this modification.

Fully modified racing Midget rear suspension features coil springs and much, much more. Not for the faint-hearted!

4 WHEELS & TYRES

Introduction

This chapter provides useful data on tyre size and speed rating, together with information on rim/tyre combinations. Also included are some pointers on converting your car to spoked wire wheels and fitting wider than standard aftermarket wheels and tyres.

Both wheels and tyres come in different widths and diameters but in all cases the standard diameter of the Sprite/Midget wheel is thirteen inches. Rim width is normally 4 inches (101.6mm) or 4.5 inches (114.3mm). Normal tyre width is 145.

Before looking at tyres for the Sprite/Midget it is important to look at the wheel and the all important rim width. Your car will have either pressed steel or wire wheels or later Rostyle wheels, assuming you haven't

already changed them for non standard items. If you are looking to use any tyre width greater than 155 then a wider wheel should be considered. Any change of wheel to one wider than the standard rim width on the Sprite/Midget is difficult, as it will almost certainly require wheelarch modification and I refer you to the bodywork chapter for further details.

Wider wheels

For replacement of pressed steel or Rostyle wheels there is a wide selection in both alloy and steel. Before you make your purchase consider the way the wheel is dished. Dishing is the way the offset on the wheel is set. Aftermarket wide wheels usually have the offset to the outside edge so any wheelarch flare will accommodate the new width, but check this before purchase. I got in touch with Compomotive Wheels to determine what will fit the Sprite/Midget. There is a choice of several of their wheels in 5 inch (127mm) and 5.5 inch (139.7mm) rim widths as the table (left) shows ("CX", "SL", etc are their codes for different wheel models).

Another fine wheel is the alloy Minilite replica that is retailed by Motobuild which, again, is available in either a 5 or 5.5 inch rim size. You will make your

CX 5.5x13	A	CX1357
SL 5.5x13	A	SL1355
MS 5-5.5x13	A	MS300/1 x F1 x R2
TH 5-5.5x13	A	TH300/1 x F1 x R2
CX 5-5.5x13	A	CX300/1 x F1 x R2

own choice, but whatever your final decision I recommend that you also purchase a set of locking wheel nuts to go with them as alloy wheels are attractive to thieves.

Above left: Alloy wheel styled upon the famous Minilite which was originally made from magnesium.
Above right: MWS 5.5 inch wire wheel fitted with Goodyear 175/70 NCT tyre.

Wire wheel conversion

An alternative, and one more and more people are choosing, is to convert their car from steel or alloy wheels to wire spoked items. You can do this by changing the back axle and front hubs or by purchasing a conversion kit from an MG specialist, such as the MG Owners Club. The principle point is that you cannot just swop the hubs on a bolt-on wheel car with wire wheel hubs as the halfshafts are different.

Another alternative is to fit bolt-on wire wheels which are available from Motor Wheel Service (MWS).

The drawback with wire wheels, though, is that you normally have to retain the standard relatively narrow rim width. However, it's possible to have wide spoked wheels made for the Sprite/Midget. The width goes up from 4 inches to 5 or 5.5 which is quite adequate for

Chrome wire wheel 3-eared knock off spinner (courtesy Victoria British Ltd).

road use. The wider wheel has an outside offset so will require wheelarch flaring. One company that can build these wheels to special order is MWS and they supply in either silver or chrome finish. MWS have worldwide distribution and their products can be purchased from Victoria British (Long Motor Corp.) and Moss Motors in the USA. Motobuild retail wide wire wheels too.

Another bonus for spoked wire wheel owners is the replacement of the standard 2-eared knock off by the MWS 3-eared type which does exactly the same job but looks smarter. If you are racing then you might want the lightest set-up which

will probably not be wire spokes, but if you do stick with wire spokes, for historic racing, than you can at least save a bit of weight by using either 2- or 3-eared specially lightened spinners which are can be supplied by Motobuild.

A final point on wheel choice relevant to the square arched Sprite/Midgets is that it can be impossible to fit certain wide wheel/tyre combinations without flaring the arch, so be warned. The practical tyre size limit is 165/70 on standard rims and less if the aftermarket wheel dishes out to any extent greater than the standard wheel.

Tyres

The subject of tyres is a big topic and, of course, I've only used a relatively small number of combinations on my own car. There are some things always worth knowing: do always use the same tyre widths front and rear as unequal widths give some undesirable, if not dangerous, handling characteristics such as sudden understeer/oversteer. Don't try and fit low profile tyres to wire spoked wheels - they are not designed for them. Do make sure the tyres you buy have an adequate speed rating for the speeds you have modified your car to attain; failure to do so can invalidate your insurance. Do check that through full spring travel and wheel lock the car has no tyre fouling on bodywork, flexible brake line or suspension components. Don't mix crossply and radial tyres on the same axle and preferably not on the car at all

Tyre selection

I sought the advice of both Goodyear and Michelin regarding tyre selection and, as well as the following tips, Goodyear provided me with a quick reference chart for rim and tyre width suitability which I have reproduced. Likewise, Michelin provided information and a diagram which 'decodes' the reference data contained on a tyre. An additional piece of information I obtained from Goodyear is the wheel revolution per mile figure for a selection of their product range which Sprite/Midget users are likely to be interested in.
The significance of this revs-per-mile figure becomes apparent when calculating speed potential for given gear ratio and differential ratio combinations. It is not important whether or not the tyres are worn in the tread, as tyres tend to 'grow' slightly

Goodyear NCT HR-rated tyre

with use due to centrifugal force and any differences between new and old tyres is negligible. I'm advised that it is generally not recommended to use tubeless type tyres with tubes, a necessity on wire spoked wheels, but I have experienced no problems whatsoever in doing so on my car. You may discover when you go to your local tyre specialist that they have never fitted tyres to wire spoked wheels and that they don't have a selection of tyres specifically designed for use with tubes. So, here are a few tips to pass on. You can advise the fitter that the inner tube should be coated with plenty of

french chalk, and inflated to its natural shape before inserting it into the wheel and tyre. This will ensure the tube is correctly positioned and in intimate contact with the tyre before final inflation. Also, it's a good idea to fit new rim tape each time you have new tyres fitted. I use black tank tape which is available from many motorsports retail outlets. A final point with spoked wire wheels is that Michelin advise in no circumstances should inner tubes be fitted with tyres of less than 65% aspect ratio. The reason for this is that problems of air trapping and chafing can lead to premature failure of the tube or even the tyre.
Should you choose to ignore the Goodyear tyre/rim chart your tyre fitter will experience severe difficulty fitting the tyre onto the rim, but it can be done. I have fitted 175 width tyres onto standard 4 inch wire spoked rims but this did produce an unpleasant sloppy feel to the car when cornering hard. Although this may sound like a moderate problem it can feel and become alarming while driving at speed through a sequence of bends.
Like wheels, your tyre choice will be down to your own personal preference. The accompanying chart is a guide to wheel/tyre combination sizes. For the record my current choice is the

Tyre size	Minimum rim width	Revs per mile	Optimum rim width	Maximum rim width
155R-13	4.00"	-	4.50" or 5.00"	5.50"
155/70R-13	4.00"	958	4.50" or 5.00"	5.50"
165/70R-13	4.50"	931	4.50" or 5.00"	6.00"
175/70R-13	5.00"	909	5.50" or 6.00"	6.00"
185/70R-13	5.00"	882	5.50" or 6.00"	6.50"
185/60R-13	5.00"	955	5.50" or 6.00"	6.50"

excellent Goodyear range of NCT tyres although I suspect the Michelin MX range of tyres would be of similar quality. Currently, I'm running the NCT 175/70R-13 on 5.5 inch wire spoked rims with very satisfying results. Previously I have been very satisfied with Uniroyals.

Tyre markings

'The writing on the wall' illustration shows all the markings which may appear on a tyre sidewall and cover both European and North American standards. The markings likely to be of most interest are those which indicate size, speed and load rating. The form of such markings is currently being changed. The outgoing markings on a radial-ply tyre of standard nominally 80% aspect ratio take the form "165 SR 13", where "165" is the tyre's nominal section width in millimetres, "S" indicates the speed rating (more of that later), "R" indicates that the tyre is radial-ply, and "13" is the nominal rim diameter in inches. A tyre with a different aspect ratio (ratio of nominal section height to section width) under this system would be marked, for instance, "165/70 SR 13" where "70" indicates a 70% aspect ratio (nominal section height 70% of nominal section width rather than the 'standard' 80%). The marking now coming into use takes the form "165/80 R 82T MXT80" where "165", "R", and "13" have the same meaning as before. "80" is the aspect status. "T" is the speed symbol. The figure "82" is the load index (of little interest to us) and "MX" is the tread pattern.

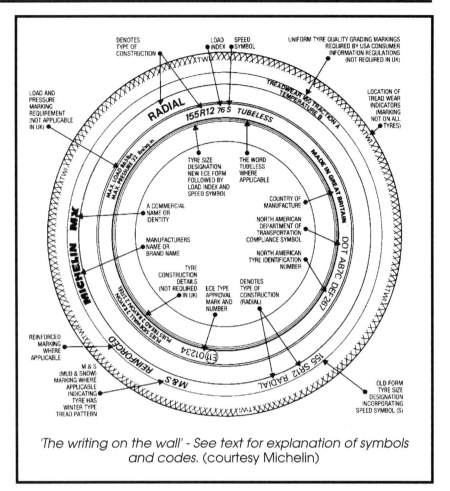

'The writing on the wall' - See text for explanation of symbols and codes. (courtesy Michelin)

The speed symbol on the tyre indicates the maximum speed at which a tyre can carry the load corresponding to its load index under specified conditions which are decoded as follows:

"Q" symbol: maximum 160km/hour (100 mph)

"R" symbol: maximum 170km/hour (106 mph)

"S" symbol: maximum 180km/hour (113 mph)

"T" symbol: maximum 190km/hour (118 mph)

"H" symbol: maximum 210km/hour (130 mph)

"V" symbol: maximum 240km/hour (150 mph)

Conclusion

A final point worth consideration is that, having sorted out your car's suspension, wheels and tyres, I thoroughly recommend you have the tracking checked, not only for safety and minimum tyre wear but simply to get the very best from your modified suspension system.

5 STEERING

Introduction

Most people don't do much with the Sprite/Midget steering as it generally works very well. However, my real gripe with the steering is the driver's lack of arm/elbow room. I'm only half an inch short of the average male height of 5' 9" (1.7 metres) and have normal length arms but have always found the steering postion awkward, with the seat as far back as it can go yet still keeping my feet on the pedals. I know that a lot of the racers use a dished wheel fitted the 'wrong' way around but I think this looks untidy so I looked for a better solution ...

Shorter column

Given that the length of the steering column controls the arm reach, I decided to have car's inner column shortened. As the safety considerations of having a column shortened are important, I went to Reco Prop who I felt I could trust to do the job for me. How much of a reduction can be achieved is not so much limited by the inner column, however, but by the steering boss. Also, the column and boss must have very near equal amounts removed. The reason for this is that the internal splines of the boss (mine any-way) are near the rear face of the boss so it's only really practi-

cal to remove an inch (25.4mm), or so, from it but the safe amount will vary from boss to boss. You certainly shouldn't remove more than half the depth of the bosses' original splines.

I sent my column away to Reco Prop and when it came back duly shortened I fitted it into the car as per the workshop manual instructions. Once the column was back in place I had the boss turned down and checked the clearance between the indicator shroud and the boss. If the space is insufficient, as mine was, it is a simple matter to cut and file the shroud to fit snugly against the boss. It only remains to fit the steering wheel back on.
CAUTION: If you do decide to shorten the inner steering column be absolutely sure that the engineering company you choose are expert welders as weld failure will result in loss of steering.

Steering wheels

There is a vast selection of steering wheels available for the Sprite/Midget and I opted for a wooden rim wheel for that authentic sixties look. The wheel is a Moto Lita item of 13 inch (330mm) diameter in a flat style. With the flat wheel and short-ened column I reckon to have achieved an extra 2 inches (50mm) of elbow room over

Left: This is the end of the steering column to shorten.

Left centre: Shortened steering column fitted in the car and steering wheel boss machined down to fit against face of indicator shroud.

that in a standard car. The smaller the diameter of the wheel you fit, the more direct (quicker) the steering becomes. The penalty is that the steering will also become heavier as the wheel becomes smaller: the answer is a sensible compromise that suits you and your car. Earlier I mentioned trimming the indicator shroud, it will, of course, also be necessary to modify the indicator stalk itself to keep it at finger tip reach. This can be done by removing the stalk and flattening out the kink till it is straight. Once this has be done it can be easily refitted.

So there you have it, a couple of simple jobs that once done will make you wonder how you ever managed without!

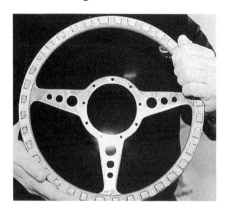

Wood-rimmed Moto Lita wheel in flat configuration gives car authentic '60s look, too.

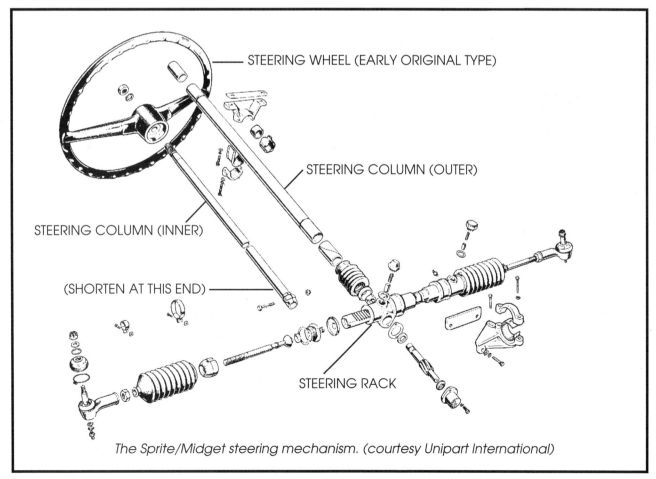

STEERING WHEEL (EARLY ORIGINAL TYPE)

STEERING COLUMN (OUTER)

STEERING COLUMN (INNER)

(SHORTEN AT THIS END)

STEERING RACK

The Sprite/Midget steering mechanism. (courtesy Unipart International)

6 ENGINE

Introduction

This is a short chapter but it should give you a useful few ideas. Although I don't have direct experience of all the ideas in this chapter, I'm satisfied that they are all workable and most are relatively straightforward and practical in their application.

Dynamo (generator) pulley

Owners of early Sprite/Midgets, like my own, will have a car equipped with a dynamo and voltage regulator control box. This is quite satisfactory for normal use but can become a minor problem with very high revving, high performance engines: the dynamo can overspeed which will lead to its destruction. The simple solution is to fit the Mini Spares reduced rpm dynamo pulley in aluminium. Richard Longman also manufactures a similar pulley but of a larger diameter and with a deeper V to prevent the fan belt jumping the pulley at very high rpm . I use the Mini Spares item on my road car and find it successfully prevents dynamo overspeeding (safe to 7600 engine rpm in my experience) and still gives an adequate charge. The Longman item is better suited to a race application as its lower gearing would not allow dynamo speeds to be high enough to

Dynamo pulleys - Longman (larger diameter) and Mini Spares.

An old shot of my car's engine bay with the radiator removed shows Mini Spares dynamo pulley in position . Also note lack of engine fan and K&N filter on engine breather outlet.

convert to an alternator which later cars and 1500cc Midgets already have as standard equipment. Aside from the obvious parts requirement, however, it's really a job for an experienced auto electrician. A s we went to press, a kit was due from a British MG specialist.

Valve timing and timing chain conversions

When you are building your engine it is well worth the minimal expense of purchasing a Kent Cams vernier cam drive which will give you infinitely variable valve timing adjustment: for further details I refer you to David Vizards *Tuning BL's A-Series Engine*. Also in the same book is the Mini Spares cogged belt drive system. Unfortunately, at the time of my engine's rebuild it was not possible to get a suitable cam drive belt system for my engine as, at that time, toothed belt drive kits did not have an engine breather in the casing. This is no longer a problem as the Mini Spares belt drive kits now have a breather built in. The Mini Spares belt kit also incorporates a vernier adjustment for precise valve timing. One of the advantages of this kit is that the removable cover, which is in two halves, allows cam timing changes to be made without having to lift the engine to get the crankshaft pulley off, unlike the standard timing gear and cover. The kit comes complete with a comprehensive set of fitting instructions which I will leave you to read yourselves should you decide to purchase

charge the battery during normal road use. Use and fitting of either pulley requires removal of the old pulley and, in either case, a slightly larger than normal fan belt will be required. I have found that even though my car is fitted with very high wattage headlamps, output from the standard dynamo with large diameter pulley is still good enough for everyday use. However, if you're going night rallying or have extra lights the Lucas C40L type dynamo will provide more output - that is if it's not already fitted.

There is an alternative to the various dynamo and pulley setups and that is quite simply to

Left: Components of Mini Spares timing belt kit. Note the oil breather outlet at top left of the main casing - this is an important feature missing from some other kits.

Above: Note bolt slots which allow precise valve timing to be achieved.

Left: Oselli rocker cover secured by Mini Spares T-nuts.

and fit this mod.

A cogged belt cam drive system gives more accurate valve timing, is capable of standing higher sustained engine speeds and is quieter in operation.

Rocker (valve) cover

There are numerous replacement rocker covers available for the A-series engine, usually made in polished alloy. I have an Oselli cover on mine as they built the engine. You might wish to fit a similarly smart alloy cover from Motobuild or use an MG Metro item. If you have a racing set-up with an oil breather from the rocker cover you may need to have a take-off from the cover fitted to allow for this. A final consideration is to replace the standard nuts with the Mini Spares T-bar securing nuts which are handy for quick access and look nice and shiny too!

Engine backplate

Motobuild or Peter May Eng. can supply an alloy engine backplate which is approximately two-thirds the weight of the standard item: a useful weight saving for the serious racer. Of course, you can always make your own as I know racer Simon Page has done.

Flywheel

David Vizard's book *Tuning BL's A-Series Engine* covers flywheel balancing and its importance. Something that is an additional consideration is the use of a Motobuild alloy flywheel for A-series and 1500-engined cars. The main body of the flywheel is in alloy but it has a steel ring gear and centre section for the clutch face (which is bolted in).

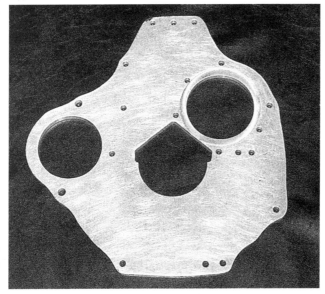

Motobuild alloy engine backplate.

Both of the steel parts are replaceable and the flywheel itself can be further lightened. If you retain a standard flywheel it is advisable to have it balanced and on race tuned 1500-engined cars this is crucial as they have been known to disintegrate. If you plan to use the AP Racing 7.5 inch clutch it is necessary to have the flywheel modified and Peter May can undertake this work. However, if your flywheel has been lightened on the clutch face by machining a large chamfer it is not possible to undertake this mod. Neither can the 7.5 inch clutch be used on the alloy flywheel and the reason for this is that the steel centre is too small. Steel flywheels are available for the 1275cc engine but have to be machined as one-off specials and I have no experience of them. I also understand that when the Morris Marina 1.3 A-series block is used the Sprite crank and flywheel are retained and the

Marina flywheel is generally discarded as being too heavy and incapable of being fitted to the Sprite crank.

Mountings & tie bars

For the racing or high performance road car Motobuild can supply competition engine and gearbox mountings made of stiffer rubber than the standard items.
Peter May Eng. fabricates engine/gearbox steady (tie) bars. These bars are rose-jointed (metal spherical joints) and prevent excessive engine movement under hard acceleration and braking.

Engine swapability

You can fit the 1275cc A-series engines into cars which had the 948 or 1098cc A-series engine with very few problems, however always transfer the larger

engine's gearbox and cooling system at the same time. If you use a 1275cc engine from a Morris Marina, you'll need to retain your Sprite/Midget engine backplate and, if possible, the crankshaft and flywheel, etc, too. It's really not worth trying to fit the Triumph 1500cc engine into cars which were equiped originally with an A-series engine - it really is a difficult conversion and you can get just as much power from an A-series.

Turbo & superchargers

I know it is possible to turbocharge the A-series engine using parts from a Metro Turbo: Simon Page's racing Turbo Frogeye is a good example (featured in the racing car chapter). I also understand that a couple of road cars with a

Simon Atherton's turbo Mk 2 Midget runs 7psi (48.2kpa) boost.

Left: Another shot of Simon's car: note fuel regulator (unfiltered type) and remote servo fitted in same place as on my own car.

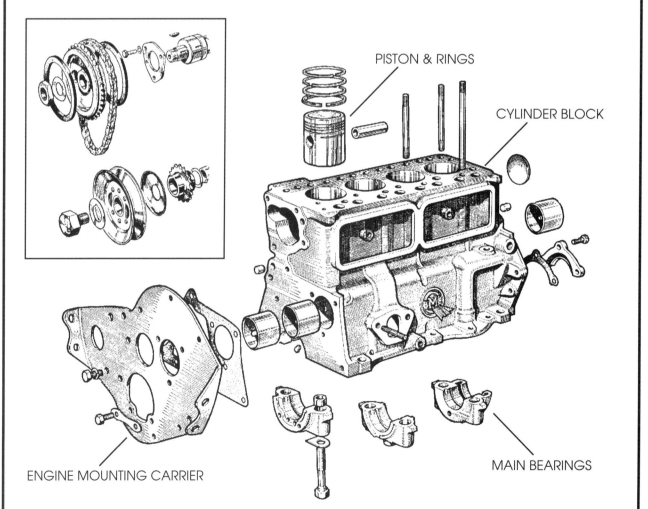

PISTON & RINGS

CYLINDER BLOCK

ENGINE MOUNTING CARRIER

MAIN BEARINGS

The original cylinder block of the Sprite MkII & III/Midget I & II. Inset details of original standard timing mechanism.

David Clarkson's supercharged 'Sprout', a green Frogeye with Shorrocks supercharger.

similar conversion are in existence as well, one being Simon Atherton's car.

Superchargers for the Sprite/Midget appear to be either Judson or Shorrocks type. The only Shorrocks blown car I know of is David Clarkson's who uses a C75 type. David's car had this mod fitted by a previous owner and the precise origin of the unit is unknown, but I imagine it was a Speedwell product and sadly now no longer available. All the Judson equipped cars I know of are in the United States of America.

The point about turbo- and supercharging the Sprite/Midget is that no specific kits seem to be available currently, so you'll need to adapt a turbo from a different model or, in the case of superchargers, install a *complete* second-hand system. In either case, you should take professional advice otherwise severe engine damage could result.

7 CARBURETTOR CONVERSIONS & FUEL INJECTION

Introduction

Most of this chapter is concerned with fitting Weber DCOE carburettors to A-series engines and will therefore be of limited interest to owners of 1500cc-engined cars: however, the general principles still apply to any DCOE carbed engine. Owners of 1500cc Midgets will be interested to know that Janspeed are one of the few companies that can supply a twin 40 DCOE Weber kit for the 1500 engine. If you're fitting Webers to a 1500 I'm told that clearance is very limited and the carbs will almost touch the brake/clutch pedal box.

This chapter also looks at other carburettor conversions and fuel injection.

Before purchasing your expensive Weber carb, manifold and filter you need to ask the question - does my engine have the power potential to merit the sidedraft Weber? If it does than read on. If you're not sure then read the carburettor chapter in David Vizard's *Tuning BL's A-series Engine* which also con-

Below: Paul Rodman's 1500cc Midget with twin DCOEs on Triumphtune intake manifold. Note ITG filter cases less filters and outer covers. (courtesy Paul Rodman)

Left: The 45 DCOE from my own 1312cc engine, fitted with 40mm chokes and utilising Goodridge braided metal petrol hose. Note blanked off servo take-off on Oselli manifold.

Below left: Janspeed 40/45 DCOE carb and manifold conversion for Sprite/Midget with neat progressive throttle linkage. (courtesy Janspeed)

tains much information on sizing and jetting.

Having decided your engine does need a sidedraft Weber the next important consideration is which size? The 40 and 45 DCOEs are the most common sizes although the DCOE is also available in 42, and the similar DCO/SP in 48 and 50. However up to 1098cc the 40 is big enough and 1275 engines usually need the bigger 45 DCOE. Rumours, at the time of writing, that the DCOE was out of production were untrue: this was confirmed by Weber Concessionaires Ltd.

Fitting a DCOE Weber

Depending on the manifold used the DCOE Weber can take up considerably more room than an SU set-up. This can make it necessary to modify the inner wing (fender) panel or even bonnet (hood) to allow room for the DCOE. If room is tight you can always use a pair of short ram pipes and a shallow K&N filter (don't try to get by without either item). My experience with an Oselli inlet manifold is that it is only the 7 x 4.5 x 3.25 inch (178 x 115 x 83mm) and 9 x 5.25 x 3.25 inch (229 x 133 x 83mm) filters that will require the special body mods that are described in the bodywork chapter.

The standard heat shields and breathers fitted to your SU set will not normally fit a Weber DCOE and manifold so they can be discarded. The breather pipe that ran from the inlet manifold to the timing case can be removed and a small K&N filter fitted to the timing cover in its place. If you are retaining the existing distributor with vacuum advance you are unlikely to find a union for the vacuum pipe on a Weber manifold. However, if you are tuning the engine to the extent of fitting a Weber DCOE you should already have considered fitting a distributor with a modified advance curve which will almost certainly not have a vacuum advance on it (see Chapter 9).

Before fitting the manifold consider whether the car will require provision for a servo vacuum take off, distributor vacuum take off or even a vacuum gauge take off, .The reason for this is that suitable unions involve drilling and tapping the manifold and this is obviously a job that should only be done with the manifold off the engine.

When fitting the manifold be sure to use a large bore competition manifold gasket if the cylinder head ports and the inlet manifold have been enlarged. Large bore manifold gaskets are available from Mini Spares Ltd.

The DCOE must be mounted with rubber O-ring type gaskets and flexible mountings. This is done to reduce fuel foaming caused by engine vibrations transmitted to the carb. Various companies market mountings

Top: Janspeed twin cable DCOE throttle linkage. (courtesy Janspeed)

Above centre: Janspeed single cable DCOE linkage modified to clear bonnet (hood) line on my own car - previously I used a bonnet with a bulge!

that get the job done.

Weber throttle linkage

A throttle linkage may be included if you buy a Weber as part of a dedicated packaged kit. Alternatively, there are lots of throttle linkages for the We-ber/A-Series combination but many of these will not fit without bonnet (hood) modifications, so check before purchase. Addi-tionally, some linkages are only suited to the transverse installa-tion of the A-series engine (Mini, Metro, etc), though these might well fit left-hand drive cars. One linkage that definitely does fit is the Janspeed item which I use on my own car, initially with a bonnet bulge but later modified by Carcraft to fit without a bulge.

Other Janspeed linkages are designed to fit with manifolds that have less or no height restrictions when used on the Sprite/Midget and present no special fitting problems.

Weber DCOE components

The following is a complete list of the components in a Weber DCOE carburettor: always use the component reference numbers quoted when ordering parts. See the accompanying illustration to match names and key numbers to components.

1	Jets inspection cover	32376.003
2	Screw securing carburettor cover	64700.001
2A	Well-bottom cover screw	64700.001
3	Gasket for jets inspection cover	41550.002 †
4	Normal washer	55510.034
4A	Normal washer	55510.034
5	Carburettor cover	31734.025
6	Gasket for carburettor cover	41715.001 †
7	Emulsion tube holder	52580.001
8	Air corrector jet	77401. *
9	Idling jet-holder	52585.006
10	Emulsion tube	61450. *
11	Idle jet	74819. *
12	Main jet	73401. *
13	Plate for carburettor bowl	52130.003
14	Choke	72116. *
15	Auxiliary venturi	69602. *
16	Dust cover	41570.001 †
17	Spring	47600.063
18	Spring retaining cover	58000.007
19	Throttle control lever	45034.044 **
20	Throttle adjusting spring	47600.007
21	Throttle adjusting screw	64590.002
22	Auxiliary venturi fixing screw	64840.003
22A	Choke fixing screw	64840.003
23	Spring washer	55525.002
23A	Spring washer	55525.002
24	Carburettor anchor nut	34705.004
24A	Nut for air intake	34705.004
25	Retaining plate for air intake	52150.004
26	Stud bolt	64955.104
27	Lock washer	55520.004
28	Hexagonal nut	34710.003
29	Gasket for cap	41640.001 †
30	Cap for bottom of bowl	32374.008
31	Carburettor body	NOT SUPPLIED
32	Spring anchor plate	52210.006
33	Spindle return spring	47605.012 †
34	Lever fixing pin	58445.001
35	Pump control lever	45082.005
36	Stud bolt	64955.007
37	Stud bolt	64955.101
38	Ball bearing	32650.001
39	Throttle securing screw	64570.006
40	Throttle valve	64005.069
41	Throttle spindle	10005.426
42	Starter control securing screw	64700.004
43	Normal washer	55510.038
44	Cap securing screw	64570.009
45	Cap for pump opening	52135.002
46	Gasket for cap	41640.021 †
47	Starter control asembly	32556.002
48	Starter control lever, complete with:	45027.030
49	Nut for screw	34720.002
50	Starter lever	45025.029
51	Cable securing screw	64800.002

52	Lever securing nut	34715.010
53	Lever return spring	47610.006
54	Cover for sheath support	32556.001
55	Starter shaft	10085.003
56	Strainer	37000.016
57	Sheath securing screw	64605.017
58	Shim washer	55555.010
59	Starter valve	64330.003
60	Spring for starter valve	47600.005
61	Spring retainer & guide	12775.004
62	Spring washer	10140.010
63	Spring retaining plate	52140/004
64	Pump control rod	10410.015
65	Spring for plunger	47600.064
66	Pump plunger	58602.003
67	Spring for idling	

	adjustment screw	47600.007 †
68	Idling adjustment screw	64750.001 †
69	Air intake horn	52840.001
70	Screw for progression	
	holes inspection	61015.002
71	Gasket for pump jet	41535.021 †
72	Pump jet	76801. *
73	Seal	41565.009 †
74	Screw plug	61015.008
75	Intake & discharge valve	79701.
76	Starter jet	75606.
77	Float	41030.00
78	Fulcrum pin	52000.001
79	Ball for valve	58300.001
80	Stuffing ball	52730.001
81	Retaining screw for	

	stuffing ball	61015.006
82	Gasket for needle valve	41535.015
83	Needle valve	79401. *
84	Gasket for union	41530.031 †
85	Spherical union	10354.001
86	Gasket for union	41530.024 †
87	Screw plug for union	12715.008
88	Strainer	37022.002
89	Gasket for filter plug	41530.024 †
90	Filter inspection plug	61002.010

* Calibrated parts
† Parts supplied in Service Kit No. 93.0015.05
** Varying with the application

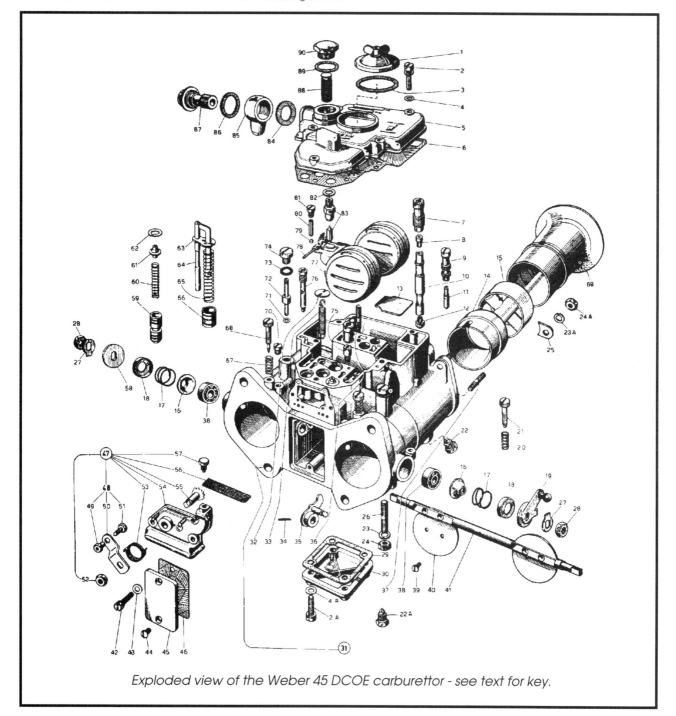

Exploded view of the Weber 45 DCOE carburettor - see text for key.

Weber calibration & operation

Once you've fitted the carburettor it will need to be provisionally calibrated. I say provisionally as the optimum settings can only be found by running the engine on a dynomometer, on which subject there is more later. The accompanying charts show basic Weber calibration for three A-series engine sizes and the 1500cc unit and should be good enough to get the car running.

Despite its precision workings the DCOE is not difficult to calibrate, though first impressions can be extremely daunting. Preliminary reading before working on the car and useful reference books are the *Haynes Weber Manual* and the *Official Weber Manual*. However, I feel that before you read any books or work on the DCOE a more rudimentary explanation of its workings is worthwhile.

Think of the DCOE as two identical carburettors in one body, because that is what it is. Don't confuse the DCOE with other Weber carbs which have one choke larger than the other, these are progressive Webers. The DCOE is a synchronized Weber, both throttle plates opening equally at once.

Like any carburettor the DCOE mixes a fuel (normally petrol (gasoline), but sometimes alcohol) with air to form a mixture which is drawn in by the engine and then burnt. The DCOE is calibrateable in very small increments to achieve the desired fuel/air requirements of your engine.

Air is sucked into the carb via the air filter and I strongly recommend you use a K&N filter as its filtering properties are unbeatable and without detriment to airflow.

Inside the air filter body are the carb trumpets/ram pipes. In nearly all instances there is a

Weber basic settings for 948cc engine

	Standard 40 DCOE Weber	Road modified 40 DCOE Weber	Race modified 40 DCOE Weber
Aux vent	4.5	4.5	4.5
Choke	31	32	33
Main jet	115	130	140
Air corr	150	155	180
Em tube	F2 or F9	F16	F16
Pump jet	35	40	40
Idle	45F9	50F2	50F2

Weber basic settings for 1098cc engine

	Standard 40 DCOE Weber	Road modified 40 DCOE Weber	Race modified 40 DCOE Weber
Aux vent	4.5	4.5	4.5
Choke	32	33	34
Main jet	120	135	145
Air corr	150	155	180
Em tube	F2 or F9	F16	F16
Pump jet	35	40	45
Idle	45F9	50F2	50F2

K&N air filter that will accommodate the ram pipes. Rams come in different sizes but normally the standard Weber rams are too long for a Sprite/Midget installation. Luckily, K&N make a variety of rams in different lengths and my experience has been that the closer you can get to the 2.55 inch (65mm) length of the standard item the better the engine will run and the larger main venturi you can use. I use a 1.53inch (39mm) ram on my

car and find that, for my engine specification, it works better than anything shorter. However, you should test different ram lengths in conjunction with chassis dyno runs to discover the optimum length for your car's engine.

In my opinion the best rams available currently are of full radius design in aluminium made by Induction Technology Ltd who can sell you a pair direct or you can get them from

Weber basic settings for 1275cc engine

	Standard 45 DCOE Weber	Road modified 45 DCOE Weber	Race modified 45 DCOE Weber
Aux vent	3.5	**3.5**	3.5
Choke	34	**36**	38
Main jet	145	**165**	175
Air corr	175	**175**	175
Em tube	F2	**F2**	F2
Pump jet	45	**50**	55
Idle	50F9	**55F9**	55F9

Weber basic settings for 1500cc engine

	Standard 40 DCOE Weber	Road modified 40 DCOE Weber	Race modified 40 DCOE Weber
Aux vent	4.5	**4.5**	4.5
Choke	28	**31**	33
Main jet	115	**125**	130
Air corr	170	**170**	170
Em tube	F16	**F16**	F16
Pump jet	35	**35**	40
Idle	45F9	**45F9**	50F9

With the very large K&N filter clearance at inner wing (fender) edge is tight.

most Weber dealers. Some fettling is required before fitting the full radius rams because, unlike the Weber and K&N rams, they have a flat base and fit against the face of the carb rather than sliding inside the carb choke. I found that one way to ensure a good fit is to cut an old Weber or K&N ram down to size to provide the necessary sleeving inside the carb: the Induction Technologies ram will then fit flush to the carb face and the sleeve. An alternative to sleeving the carb when using the full radius ram is to radius the Aux venturi and the inside edge of the carburettor.

Do not be tempted to run your engine without an air filter as engine bore wear will be excessive. Neither should you run the engine without rams because their absence will seriously degrade the performance of the engine. If you do use the full radius rams with a K&N filter only the 9 x 5.25 x 3.25/4.5/5.5 inch (229 x 133 x 83/114/140mm) bodies will accommodate them. Even then, it's necessary to re-position the internal pillars that secure the filter case lid to the outermost edge of the case. I understand that K&N can supply different stampings of the case or leave out these holes for you to drill yourself. I drilled the holes myself and simply blanked off the old ones with insulating tape.

A final point to note is that whatever ram and filter case combination you use make sure that you have at least 1.18 inch (30mm) between the end of the ram and the filter case, especially on K&N cases, as less clearance will impede airflow. Once air has flowed through the ram pipe it enters the two venturis in each choke tube, first the auxiliary venturi where the airflow draws fuel mixture from the main jet ways. The auxiliary venturi acts like a signal amplifier because its end is positioned at the point of greatest depression in the main venturi. (Sometimes the auxiliary venturi is

Operation of the Weber DCOE carburettor.
(courtesy Weber Concessionaires Ltd)

Figure 1

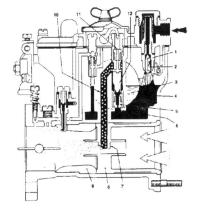

Figure 2

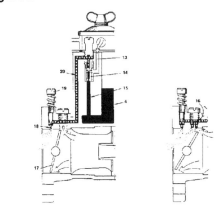

Figure 3

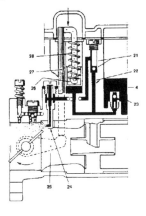

Figure 4

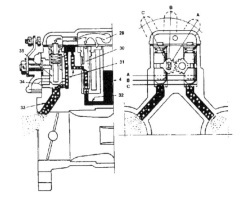

NORMAL OPERATION – Fig. 1
The fuel arrives through the needle valve (**1**) to the bowl (**4**) where the float (**3**) controls the opening of the needle (**2**) in order to maintain a constant fuel level. Through the ducts (**6**) and the main jets (**5**), it reaches the emulsion tubes (**12**) from which after having been mixed with the air coming from the air corrector jets (**11**), through the pipes (**10**) and the nozzles (**7**) it reaches the carburation area consisting of the auxiliary venturis (**8**) and chokes (**9**).

ACCELERATION – Fig. 3
By closing the throttle valves, the lever (**25**), by means of the shaft (**27**), lifts the piston (**26**). The fuel is thus drawn from the bowl (**4**) into the pump cylinder through the valve (**23**). By opening the throttles, the shaft (**27**) is free and the piston (**26**) is pushed down under the action of the spring (**28**); by means of the ducts (**22**) the fuel is injected through the delivery valve (**21**) to the pump jets (**24**) into the carburettor throats. The inlet valve (**23**) is provided with a calibrated hole which discharges the excess fuel delivered by the accelerating pump into the float bowl.

IDLING OPERATION AND PROGRESSION PHASE – Fig. 2
The fuel is carried from the bowl (**4**) to the calibrated holes of the idling jets (**14**) through the ducts (**15**). Emulsified with the air coming from the ducts (**13**), through the ducts (**20**) and the idling feed holes (**18**), adjustable by means of screws (**19**), the fuel reaches the carburettor throats below the throttles (**17**). From the ducts (**20**) the mixture can reach the carburettor throats also through the progression holes (**16**).

COLD START DEVICE – Fig. 4
The fuel flowing from the bowl (**4**) is fed to the cold start device through the ducts (**32**) and the starting jets (**30**). Emulsified with the air coming from the hole (**29**) it reaches the opened valves (**35**) through the ducts (**31**) and, further emulsified by air entering from orifices (**34**), is then carried by means of the ducts (**33**) to the carburettor throats below the throttles.
Engine cold start – choke fully on – position 'A'
Engine half-warm start – choke half on – position 'B'
Engine normal running – choke knob must be pushed back as soon as the engine has reached the operating temperature – position 'C'

Left: Comparison between full radius and standard type ram tubes - both 39mm.

Centre left: Full radius ram tube with sleeve for carb.

Bottom left: Paul Rodman's 1500cc Midget with twin DCOEs - note marginal inner wing clearance with filter bodies fitted. (courtesy Paul Rodman)

known as the booster venturi). The air (and now fuel mix) having passed through the auxiliary venturi, passes through the main venturi where it speeds up due to the aerodynamic shape (convergent/divergent) of the venturi. Because fuel is drawn into the airstream by the partial vacuum in the venturi, once the fuel flow starts it is difficult to control the flow precisely, and this can cause excessive enrichment of the mixture. With fixed jet carbs such as the DCOE this problem is overcome in part by having a main jet system with air correction. The air correction on the DCOE is controlled by an air correction jet which allows air to be drawn in with the fuel and, in a similar manner, by the holes in the emulsion tube. The main jet and air correction are supplemented by the idle jet system which provides appropriate fuel air mixtures at engine idle and low speeds. The main system provides fuel air mixture at larger throttle openings and stays in use all the way to full throttle; more of this later.

To improve performance the main fuel supply system is supplemented by an accelerator jet known as the pump jet. The pump jet shoots liquid fuel into the venturis when the throttle is suddenly opened and also streams extra fuel when the throttle is in the fully open position.

Now that you understand the basic principles of how the DCOE works, a more detailed

*Left: Induction Technologies'
(ITG) full radius ram in 39mm size
just fits inside the filter case.*

*Centre left: K&N filter with full
radius rams and re-positioned
cover support pillars.*

*Bottom left: Looking into the
DCOE, again, note filter cover
pillars.*

look at the three mixture con-
trolling areas completes the
overall explanation.

The idle system is regulated by
one component but this comes
in a combination of jet hole size
and emulsion hole size (emulsion is the mixing of the fuel with
the air to form fuel droplets
suspended in air). So this single
component has two
calibrateable properties. Small
adjustments to the idle system
can be made by using the idle
mixture adjustment screw.
Remember that, for the main
part, when the idle system is
working the main system is not
and vice versa, so they work
independently of each other.
The only, and obvious, exception to this is the overlap period
when one system is finishing
and the other starting.

The main system is similar to the
idle system but has three
calibrateable components.
Unlike the idle system they are
removable separately. The
three parts are the main jet,
emulsion tube and air corrector.
They all fit together with a
holder to form one component.
The accelerator pump jet is
calibrated by a jet, spring and
a spill-back or bleed valve but
largely by jet because for most
if not all A-series applications
the spill-back valve in the float
bowl will be closed. Whilst the
primary function of the accelerator pump is to supply a jet of
fuel for sudden acceleration, it
can affect the main mixture
strength as petrol is drawn from
it at high engine speeds but, as
explained above, for the A-
series engine the spill-back
valve is most likely to be closed.

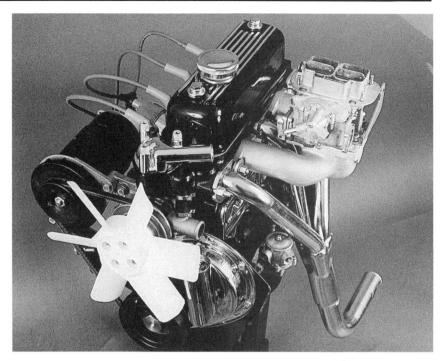

The Weber DGV (DGAV) conversion for the A-series engined Sprite/Midget as retailed in the USA by Victoria British Ltd. (courtesy Victoria British Ltd)

However, on 1500 Midget applications this is not likely to be the case.

Earlier I mentioned the venturis which come in different sizes to suit the airflow and power demand of the engine. Changes in venturi size will need to be balanced by mixture strength changes to keep the air/fuel ratio correct.

Before starting the engine for the first time with the DCOE note the sizes of all calibrated components, like jets, and keep a record every time you make a calibration change. The Weber manuals are illustrated so there is no reason for not checking all the components.

The dyno IS THE ONLY WAY you can set the calibration correctly. Choose a dyno operator who is familiar with the DCOE and holds stocks of jets etc. The first time I took my car to a chassis dyno with a DCOE carb with a well-set up DCOE, I still saw a gain of 10BHP on changing main jets! Remember there is no such thing as a pre-set DCOE carb and jetting recommendations in any book will be just that - recommendations. That really wraps up the DCOE Weber conversion. If you come across an unusual problem you can always seek advice from your dealer but if you read the manuals and follow the fitting instructions in this chapter and the manuals you shouldn't have any problems.

Weber 32/36 DGV (DGAV) conversion

Just as this book was going to press I learnt that a popular conversion in the USA is to fit the Weber 32/36 DGV (DGAV) two barrel progressive downdraft carburettor. I have no experience of this conversion whatsoever but, from the photos I've seen, it does look as if bonnet (hood) clearance might be a problem, requiring a substantial bulge to clear the carb. Aside from possible height problems this would appear to be a good conversion. The DGV (DGAV) is a very common and functional carb fitted to many Ford engines and might well work out a cheaper option than a DCOE conversion, given its second-hand availability. Victoria British Ltd in the USA are one company who I know retail this conversion kit. I would, of course, be interested to hear from any reader who has experience of this conversion.

SU HS4 conversion

You can convert your car from the standard one and a quarter inch SUs to one and a half inch SU HS4 units. The carbs and manifold are available from Janspeed Engineering who will also be able to advise on calibration for your engine.

Fuel injection conversion

I'm not aware of anybody running a fuel injected Sprite/Midget yet but it seems likely that systems will be adapted to the cars in the near future by those seeking ultimate performance or needing to comply with particularly onerous emission standards.

In the meantime, if you have a DCOE equipped car it should be possible to fit Weber's Alpha electronic engine management, fuel injection and integrated ignition system. I understand the system successfully reduces harmful emissions, reduces fuel consumption and improves overall driveability but doesn't make much difference to top end power. Unfortunately, the Alpha kits were expensive at the time of writing.

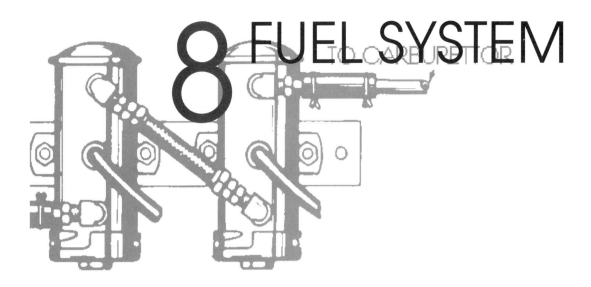

8 FUEL SYSTEM

Introduction

If you have modified your car's engine to produce more power you will have also discovered that more fuel is required to produce that power. My own once humble Sprite now delivers an average 20mpg but it does develop considerably more power, with its 45 DCOE Weber carburettor, than a standard engine. It's wise to check that the car is actually burning the fuel and not simply leaking it. Once your'e sure the fuel system is leak-free, the engine should be tuned and the carb(s) calibrated, preferably on a rolling road dynomometer. The operator should ask you how you will be using the car and calibrate the carb appropriately. For instance, a race car may need a much richer fuel mixture than a road or fast road car.

If your car's modified engine is not to suffer from fuel starvation (symptoms may show during dyno testing), you'll need to uprate the fuel delivery system's capacity until it can cope with the maximum fuel flow required.

Fuel pumps

The standard electric pump can only cope with moderate increases in fuel demand and that's assuming it's in good working order. Depending on the state of your engine's tune the easiest and cheapest way to ensure good fuel supply may be to simply fit a brand new standard pump. In some cases a similar pump from a different model with a large engine may have the extra capacity to cope with the extra horsepower of your engine. Another solution is to fit two standard pumps to run in series.

For really serious horsepower the answer is to fit a competition fuel pump. On 1500cc-engined cars the mechanical pump can be discarded and the casting for the pump fitting in the block can either be blocked off or used as an additional engine breather - either way this will require the fabrication of a small plate. On A-series-engined cars the high capacity competition pump will simply replace the existing electric pump.

Shopping for a competition pump can be more than a little bewildering to say the least. A great many people will be only too quick to sell you a pump which might do the job. On the other hand, it might still not match your requirements or it might even represent overkill. One of the things to watch with a pump is the pressure it generates. Just because the pump can produce 7psi (48.3kpa) - which doesn't sound much - it doesn't mean your car's carb can handle it. The *Weber Tuning Manual* tells us that the

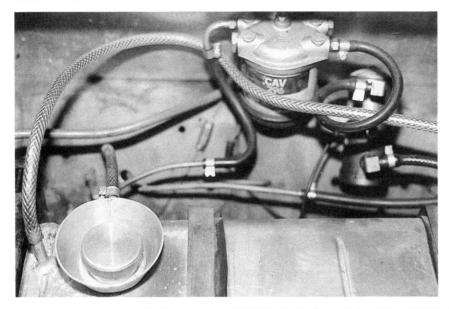

Left: Boot-mounted fuel tank with Lucas fuel filter and Interrupter fuel pump. A high pressure pump with regulator in engine bay completes the fuel delivery system of Simon Page's turbo Frogeye.

fuel line but, believe me, it's not. I can relate an experience that I hope will convince you of it's advantages ...
After having some bodywork modifications done on my car at a small body shop, I drove the car towards home. On the way I stopped for fuel and popped the bonnet (hood) to check the engine oil; the en-

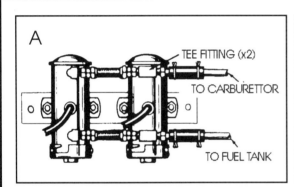

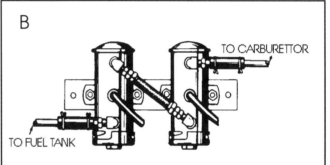

Fuel pumps can be plumbed in parallel (A) for twice the fuel flow at the same pressure, or in series (B) for twice the pressure and normal flow. (courtesy Facet Enterprises Inc)

average Weber likes between 2.8psi (19.3kpa) and 4.2psi (29kpa) minimum and maximum respectively. Unfortunately, it's not that simple as the actual flow rates also have to be considered. My suggestion is to 'phone an expert supplier and ask for advice. One expert I can recommend are Facet (UK) Concessionaires (FSE). They are the main importers for the range of Interrupter pumps that just about everyone will try and sell you so they know what they're talking about.

Fuel regulators

Establishing the best pump for your engine isn't the end of your

problem. Because of the high pressure output that goes with the high flow pump you will most likely need a fuel regulator as well, if you haven't already got one fitted. The regulator will have a pressure adjusting facility which should be set to suit the fuelling requirements of your car. Your retailer, or Facet, can advise on the best setting for your particular application. Facet supply two types of regulator: one with push fitting connections for normal petrol hose, or a more recent type that has threaded fittings. The threaded fitting type is to be preferred as it will allow the use of braided metal hose for the fuel line. Braided metal hose may sound like a luxury for the

gine was stopped but the ignition on. There was a small

The latest FSE-retailed fuel regulator and filter.

Top right: FSE-retailed regulator on my car with Goodridge hose and fittings.

Above: Paul Rodman's modified 1500cc Midget again. Note tidy positioning of fuel regulator on a homemade bracket.

cloud of steam coming from somewhere very near the car's 3-into-1 exhaust manifold and closer investigation revealed that the steam was, in fact, fuel vapour and the plastic petrol pipe was melting on the exhaust. A hasty engine switch off prevented a big and unpleasant bang. How had this happened? Quite simply, when the panel beater fitted the inner wing (fender) he had moved the petrol pipe and then forgotten to re-fix it in its original position. It's an incident I'll never forget.

If your tuning route was by the use of either super-or turbocharging you have a host of other considerations concerning fuel pressure and induction boost. Not least of these will be whether you need to have a special seal kit for the carb. There are a whole host of variables to consider and, again, I suggest you seek expert advice, having full details of your mods to hand.

With your new high capacity pump and regulator (which is also likely to incorporate a filter), you're almost there. A final small but vital consideration is the bore of the petrol pipes, both rigid and flexible. There's not much point spending a lot of money on an efficient pump and regulator only to restrict fuel flow with skinny pipes. Choose a realistic pipe bore according to your engine's needs. A lot of pumps have special unions and I assume your retailer sold you the relevant ones to go with the pump. However, it may be worth considering a braided metal hose and union kit. Goodridge can supply your needs if you give them details of fittings and length of hose required.

So finally, it's time to fit the pump, fuel lines and regulator

Below: FSE Bendix type pump on my car mounted on rubber mounts; once more, Goodridge hose and fittings are put to use.

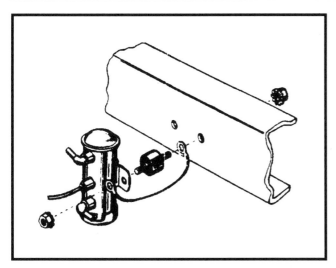

I recommend the electric pump is fitted on rubber mounts as shown here. (courtesy Facet Enterprises Inc)

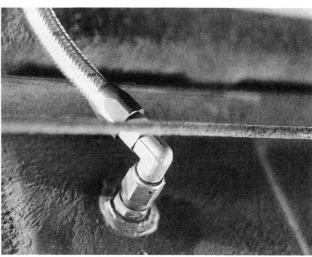

Goodridge hose and fittings at fuel tank union on my car: this was the only way I could think of to run a large bore fuel line right up to the tank.

to the car. Ideally, the pump should be fitted as near the fuel tank as possible and this is not difficult on the Sprite/Midget as siting can be quite near the original electric pump. On 1500cc cars try and fit the pump as near the fuel tank as possible. It may seem like a good idea to fit the fuel pump under the bonnet but in practice this does not work as well: the reason for this is that the engine bay air temperatures are on the warm side which can cause fuel vaporisation problems. Where you finally decide to mount the pump will be up to you, but make sure you follow the guidance contained with the pump fitting instructions.

Pumps can be noisy and some models are available with noise reducing rubber mountings. Once the pump, pipes and regulator are installed the only remaining job is to wire in the pump. Again, your application will decide the way the pump should be wired. It may be a simple job of using the existing pump connections. If, however, you are wiring the pump to a separate switch and not through the ignition, be sure to mark that switch(es) suitably. FSE can also sell you a safety shut-off switch: a single pole, double throw pressure switch which is connected into the pump's electrical supply. Activation is by engine oil pressure,

so stalling the engine shuts off the pump. This is worth considering if you are going to do a lot of motorsport with your car or simply as an added safety feature. Another piece of electronics which may be of interest is a RPM switched relay. This is a 'black box' from Microdynamics that can be used to switch on an auxiliary fuel pump (for the racer) or a nitrous oxide system.

With the new fuel system parts fitted run the engine (outdoors) and check for leaks. Then, and only then, test the car either on a rolling road dynomometer or race circuit to ensure fuel starvation has been eliminated.

9 IGNITION SYSTEM

Introduction

If you've read David Vizard's book *Tuning BL's A-series Engine* you'll probably have a fairly hot motor in your Sprite/Midget: you may even have done some of the ignition system mods that the book suggests. Maybe your car still has a standard engine and you wish to uprate the ignition for ease of maintenance and performance gain. Either way, this chapter will give you my experience of the A-series ignition system and how to obtain enhanced reliability and performance.

When in good condition the standard ignition system is more than adequate for the standard engine. However, an engine tuned or modified for greater street performance or to competition standards is more demanding in its ignition requirements. The larger volumes of fuel/air mixture, often at higher compression that are burnt in tuned engines will require a higher voltage at the spark plugs to ensure complete combustion and higher engine revolutions per minute (RPM) require more sparks per minute. The total voltage that can be delivered to the spark plug is the main factor governing whether or not the plugs fire

Micro Dynamics Formula One contact breaker points-triggered electronic ignition system with built-in rev limiter.

successfully. Voltage shortfalls at the plug can be attributed to coil output, losses due to resistance in the HT leads and, finally, the spark plugs themselves can also limit spark quality and strength if their initial resistance is too high.

Modification options

This chart indicates the desirability of each modified component but, with ignition systems, it is really a case of evaluating and meeting the ignition demands of the engine as you modify it. Nonetheless, the guide may help you decide your priorities.

Fit new contact breaker points and condenser to your existing ignition set-up and take a hard look at the rotor arm and distributor cap.

Intended usage	check spark plug heat range	High perf. ignition (HT) leads	Electronic ignition system	High output sports coil	Rev limiter
Std/mild road	No/yes	No	Desirable	No	No
Fast road	Yes	Yes	Yes (contact-less best)	Yes	Desirable
Comp.	Yes	Yes	Yes (contact-less best)	Yes	Yes

Spark plugs

Every spark plug has an initial resistance due mostly to the gap. The current will flow until the electrical voltage applied arcs across that gap. The current passes through the central electrode which, in standard plugs, is made of nickel alloy. An electrode which has less resistance will produce a stronger spark so both NGK and Bosch manufacture plugs with copper and platinum central electrodes as copper and platinum are excellent electrical conductors offering minimal resistance.

Perhaps equally important to engine and ignition performance is the grade of plug you use and, once again I refer you to *Tuning BL's A-series Engine* by David Vizard. For the record my preference is for the NGK BPES or BPEV series of plugs, though I have found that I have not been able to get much more than 9,000 miles (15,000km) from a set and, apparently, this is only to be expected when plugs are used in a high performance engine with a good

ignition system. A point to note is that high performance engines like colder (hard) rated plugs. The heat rating of the plug will be the key decision to make so, if you are trying to find the optimum heat range plugs for your car, start with cold plugs and work towards warmer ones, that way no harm will be done to the engine. Note that

NGK BP8ES and BP8EV plugs: note protruded tip which is indicated in the plug marking by the "P". (courtesy NGK)

Champion and NGK use numbers that progress in the opposite directions in relation to heat range so be sure the tuning shop understands your need. Plugs which are too hot for the engine will create pre-ignition knocking after or during hard use and may cause the engine to run on after it is switched off. Prolonged use of plugs which are too hot can damage the Sprite/Midget engine.

Ignition (HT) leads

HT leads also have some resistance to electrical current. Most Sprite/Midget leads are manufactured from carbon impregnated string, which has the highest resistance value and which, after about 20,000 miles (30,000km) no longer function very efficiently. The best of the available alternatives is the wire wound, inductively suppressed HT lead and, as direct replacements, such leads deliver the highest energy to the plug. Amongst the better grades of leads I can recommend are those supplied by Micro Dynamics Ltd or NGK Ltd.

Sports coil

By making the best of plug and lead choices the ignition system

Right: A close look at an installed Dynorite contactless (does not use contact breaker points) module with ballast resistor.

is now capable of delivering the full potential of the standard ignition coil. To create a higher voltage a high output sports coil is required. High output coils have a greater number of secondary windings than standard which produces a greater voltage as the contact breakers open.

Several manufacturers produce sports coils suitable to use as direct replacements for the standard item. The drawback with a sports coil is that it takes more current and can increase contact breaker points arcing which leads to higher erosion and the need for more frequent points resetting and renewal.

Rev limiter

This device cuts ignition pulses at a pre-set engine speed to prevent engine over-revving. Microdynamics produce an engine cut-out that is available either separately or incorporated into an electronic ignition system. It is called "Smooth Cut" because it works electronically

rather than mechanically and will not cut the ignition completely when it comes into operation.

Electronic ignition systems

The advantage of so-called "electronic" ignition systems is that they remove most of the vagaries associated with mechanical (points and advance mechanism) spark timing. However, electronic systems come with many different features. I have

used the Microdynamics Formula One electronic ignition system for some years and, initially, one advantage of the system was that it was a contact breaker points triggered system and could be fitted to the car without having the distributor advance mechanism altered. If you have a highly tuned engine in your car you may well have moved on to a different distributor such as an Aldon or Microdynamics item which has an advance curve adjusted to suit your engine's state of tune and the ignition system the engine is using. Since original fitment I have progres-

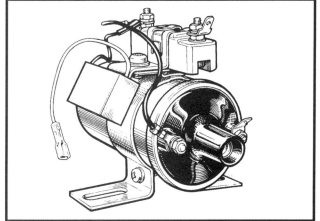

The Microdynamics Macro Spark high peformance ignition coil with ballast resistor (not fitted to later models) and cold starter adaptor. (courtesy Microdynamics)

The Microdynamics fully electronic, contact breakerless distributor now used on my car.

sively upgraded the Miicrodynamics system into a fully electronic package; this involved having the distributor rebuilt and another ignition package fitted to drive the distributor electronics in conjunction with the existing system. During the rebuild of the distributor I took the opportunity to have its ignition advance and retard system re-curved to take advantage of previous rolling road information on the ignition advance demands of my car's tuned engine . When you read the rolling road chapter you'll find further comment on optimising ignition curves.

I don't intend giving precise installation instructions as the various systems and system combinations available present too many possibilities; however, you may find the following useful. For the most part the coil can remain in its original location. I have mounted ignition system 'black boxes' both on the pedal box cover and inner wing without any problems but bear in mind that the main consideration for siting ignition electronic units is of course to keep wiring runs short and, simultaneously, keep the units away from excessive heat, dampness or vibration.

Ignition system modifications to my own car started off with a Miicrodynamics coil and distributor, then a rev limited points triggered system and, finally, to a contactless system and I suggest that this step-at-a-time method is a good route to take. One of the beauties of the Microdyamics and some other ranges is that there is this scope to expand and continually upgrade the system.

Conclusion

My final comment is that although the ignition system may never gain you new horsepower, a poorly maintained or inadequate set-up will always

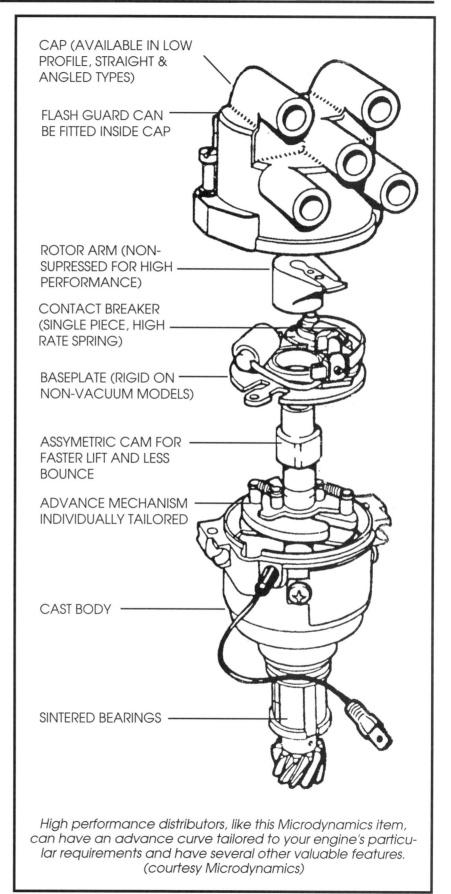

CAP (AVAILABLE IN LOW PROFILE, STRAIGHT & ANGLED TYPES)

FLASH GUARD CAN BE FITTED INSIDE CAP

ROTOR ARM (NON-SUPRESSED FOR HIGH PERFORMANCE)

CONTACT BREAKER (SINGLE PIECE, HIGH RATE SPRING)

BASEPLATE (RIGID ON NON-VACUUM MODELS)

ASSYMETRIC CAM FOR FASTER LIFT AND LESS BOUNCE

ADVANCE MECHANISM INDIVIDUALLY TAILORED

CAST BODY

SINTERED BEARINGS

High performance distributors, like this Microdynamics item, can have an advance curve tailored to your engine's particular requirements and have several other valuable features. (courtesy Microdynamics)

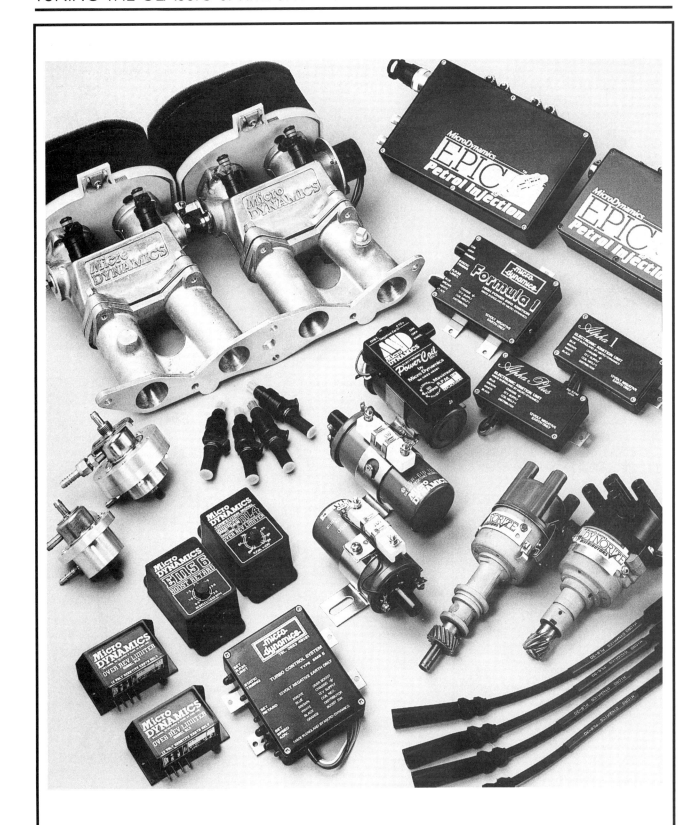

Whatever your ignition requirements, the Microdynamics range is wide enough to meet your precise needs: they produce fuel injection systems, too!

The Formula One system installed on the inner wing of my Sprite with the Dynorite contactless ignition module on the pedal box cover.

lose horsepower. Perhaps more importantly, an efficient ignition system will provide good starting combined with reliability and minimum maintenance.

10 COOLING SYSTEM

Introduction

Of the heat energy produced by an internal combustion engine about a third is dissipated by the cooling system. Without cooling the engine would overheat, and seize its internals. An engine tuned to produce more power will also produce more heat and whilst the Sprite/Midget cooling system can handle moderate increases in engine power before becoming overstretched, you will need to uprate the system for serious high performance use. For maximum engine power the best coolant temperature is about 149° F (65° C) which is quite a bit lower than normal, but unless you're aiming for competition use it's not necessary to achieve this low a running temperature.

Though this chapter is designed to help improve the Sprite/Midget cooling system for tuned cars, I have not provided a modification options table for this Chapter as the modification combinations are diverse with no natural priorities.

Radiator/s

Lowering the coolant temperature of the engine's cooling system is best achieved by increasing airflow through the radiator, improving the speed and volume of coolant circulation through the engine or, to a lesser extent, increasing the coolant capacity. Auxiliary radiators, which will increase coolant capacity and expose the coolant to more airflow, are available from manufacturers such as Serck or you could use an old heater element to increase the radiator area of your system. Alternatively, to achieve the same objectives, you might choose to have a specially large radiator made: Serck competition dept will be able to make such a unit for you if this is the route you decide to take. Fitting will require fabricated brackets to suit your unit and siting will be in any position where there is good airflow.

Engine-driven cooling fans

If you want to reduce the water temperature by increasing airflow through the radiator during traffic/slow speed use the best way is too fit a more effective cooling fan.

An engine-driven fan nearly always produces the highest airflow figures and the range of engine-driven fans for the Sprite/Midget come in two-bladed and up to sixteen bladed sizes. An electric fan will never be as effective as a multi bladed engine-driven fan at high engine rpm but the electric fan will push or draw more air through the radiator when the engine is ticking over in traffic or running at low rpm. It is possible to keep the engine fan and have a Kenlowe electric fan for auxiliary cooling, but more about electric fans later. I feel any cooling solution should only have one fan for no better reason than it is neater.

Thermostats and blanking sleeves

There is a thermostat in the cooling system to allow the engine to reach its operating temperature quickly by cutting off water circulation to the radiator. Thermostats are made to open at a specific temperature which varies with the requirements of the cooling system.

It's possible to get a thermostat that will open between 149° and 158° F (65° to 70° C) as opposed to the more usual 158° F (70° C) or even as high as 176° F (80° C). A change to a lower temperature opening thermostat will tend to reduce normal running temperature of an engine providing the radiator's capacity to cool has been increased as described earlier. Alternatively the thermostat can be removed and a blanking

A-series engine blanking sleeve.

Goodridge metal braided hose can be used for water lines, too.

sleeve substituted; at the same time also remove the bypass hose and plug the fittings on the head and water pump. Unless you have the head off the engine I suggest fitting the blanking plugs to two by-pass hoses and fitting one hose to the water pump, the other to the block. Blanking sleeves and plugs can be obtained from Oselli Engineering Ltd., Mini Spares and other A-series engine specialists The point of the so-called 'blanking sleeve' is not to block the flow of water, but instead to divert it to create better distribution of coolant around the whole engine: for further details see *Tuning BL's A-series Engine* by David Vizard. If your'e fitting a new pump get the later Mini Metro item which does not have the bypass hose fitting of earlier pumps.

Electric fans

Having dropped the water temperature by one or more of the previously described methods, the engine-driven fan is generally redundant as the water temperature is usually cool enough without further assistance, except in slow traffic. The substitution of the engine-driven fan by an electric fan will restore the temperature level by switching on as re-

quired - either by thermostat switching or driver controlled switching. An added bonus of using an electric fan is that removal of the engine-driven fan can release an extra couple of BHP.

Kenlowe make a purpose built electric fan kit for the Sprite/Midget with a 10 inch (254mm) fan, there are also several universal electronic fan kits. For my car I chose the 327-8 universal fitting 12 inch (305mm) thermostatic fan, though any kit with a 10 inch (254mm) fan will be adequate for most uses. Fitting a universal fan kit is more involved than fitting one of the fans specifically designed for the Sprite/Midget. Kenlowe fans have comprehensive fitting instructions but here are a few details specific to fitting the big 12 inch (305mm) universal thermostatic fan to the Sprite/Midget.

Remove the standard engine-driven fan and re-bolt the water pump pulley back onto the pump using shorter bolts. Detach the radiator and cowl and

Top brackets for radiator are homemade - note size of electric fan.

cut the cowl to leave just the bottom section or fabricate your own brackets. The top of the radiator will need to be supported by fabricated brackets anyway, which are very simple to make from sheet or strip steel or aluminium. This done you can refit the radiator. Not only have you now made room for the big fan but also increased airflow to the engine bay which is no bad thing. Note that the fan should be fitted to the forward face of the radiator.

Kenlowe offer two types of universal fitting. The first is the V-mounting that attaches the fan direct to the radiator matrix (Unifan type) and the other the adjustable bars system upon which the fan is mounted (thermostatic). I strongly recommend the adjustable bars system even though it can take a little longer

Electric fan fitted to remains of bottom radiator cowl.

to fit.

The Kenlowe fan kit comes with a thermostatic switch which controls it, however, my preference is manual control via a dashboard mounted switch which is illuminated when in the "On" position. With a manual switch you can start the fan running the moment you enter traffic rather than let the engine get hot enough to operate a thermostatic switch.

Whichever switching method you employ be sure the fan is pushing the air through the radiator. If you reverse the connections the fan will try to suck air through the radiator against the airflow of the car and the water temperature will soar.

Radiator & expansion tank caps

Like most cooling systems the

Sprite/Midget cooling system operating pressure is determined by the radiator cap and different models have cooling systems with different operating pressures. The range is from 4psi (27.58kpa) to 15psi (103.5kpa) although the most common rates are 7 and 13psi (47.26-89.63kpa). By pressurising the system the coolant's boiling point is raised. Each 1 pound per square inch (6.9kpa) of pressure will raise the boiling point by 3° F. Not only does this allow the running temperature to be raised well above boiling point, it also effectively allows the use of a smaller radiator.

I use a 13psi (89.63kpa) rad cap on my own Sprite cooling system which is the standard rating. If you have an earlier model which uses a lower rated cap you can use a higher rated cap to provide a safety margin.

Another view of the electric fan/radiator/cowl assembly.

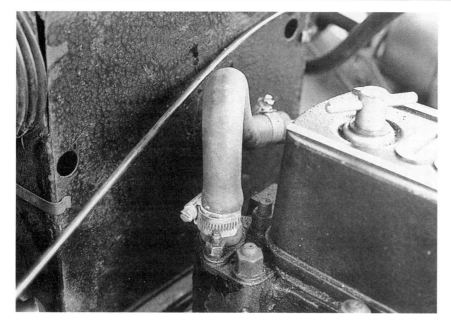

Direct hose fitting in lieu of heater tap, this hose bypasses the heater matrix (which is removed from heater box).

amount of power from the engine.

It is suggested that you retain the standard pump and only fit an alternative if all other methods of increased cooling capacity fail to give the desired result. Conversely, if the engine is overcooled you could fit a pump of smaller capacity than the standard unit.

Once coolant has been expelled from the system's overflow (assuming no overflow tank is fitted) in heavy traffic or sitting on the start line at a race it cannot be replaced until the system has had time to cool down. Once on the move again a system that has a reduced capacity is even more likely to run hot and lead to further coolant loss etc.

If you do use a higher rated radiator cap than standard it can create problems for the system by blowing out the core plugs in the block or causing leaks at hose joints and this is something that needs to be closely watched.

Heater and heater tap

An option when modifying the cooling system is whether or not to retain the heater element. I consider retention unnecessary when the system has been modified by fitting a blanking sleeve as the heater blower can still extract enough warm air

from the engine bay for demisting without the element.

Racers may wish to keep the heater element, but for reasons outlined in Chapter 18, it will be necessary to relocate the unit. If you do remove the element, retain the heater tap but reverse its position so that it will be easy to run a hose from the tap to the union at the front of the engine. NEVER turn off the heater tap as this action will create overheating of number 4 cylinder.

Water pumps

With the A-series engine there are quite a few alternative water pumps to choose from as most of the later Metro pumps will fit the Sprite/Midget, as will most Mini pumps, although it's not necessary to get a high capacity water pump just because you have a high power output engine. The requirement is for the smallest capacity pump that will get the job done and sap the least

Conclusion

As you will have realised by now, there are many ways to modify the cooling system and the options you select will depend on the use to which you intend to put your car. In some cases a car that is raced and used as a road car may have to compromise, as the best set-up for racing may leave the road temperatures on the cool side, though this could be remedied with a radiator blind. In winter it's possible to end up with an engine running too cool and the cure again is too partially blank off the radiator.

Finally, if the radiator or hoses are leaky and suspect; you'll never succeed in keeping the water temperatures down so start with a good, well maintained system and work on improving it and you will get good results. Remember that failure to achieve proper cooling for a high performance engine could result in permanent damage to the engine.

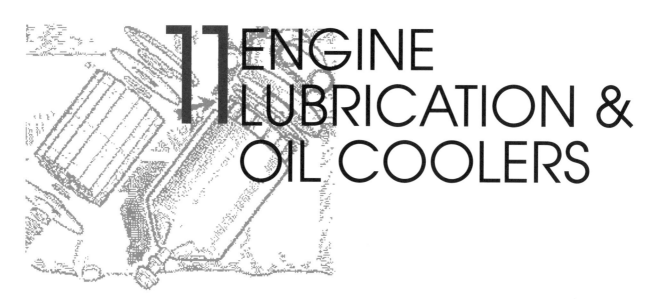

11 ENGINE LUBRICATION & OIL COOLERS

Introduction

Engine oil is not only a lubricant, but also a coolant. A high engine temperature will produce a high oil temperature, the oil dissipating approximately 10-15% of engine heat. As the engine oil becomes hotter it gets thinner and consequently less protective, so obviously oil choice and temperature are important. A cheap oil will break down more quickly at high temperatures and the very best (and most expensive) protection will come from a good synthetic oil.

I use Mobil One synthetic as it has a reputation for being among the best. This oil will withstand temperatures of up to 320° F (150° C) though I understand that oil temperatures between 203° F (95° C) and 230° F (110° C) will produce the best engine power output. To ensure your engine is running at the optimum oil temperature you will need to monitor it by fitting an oil temperature gauge. Once fitted (see instruments chapter) you will be able to determine the cooling requirements for your engine. As in previous chapters, here is a guide to modifications to your car.

Engine Lubrication options

The accompanying chart shows the author's engine lubrication recommendations for the Sprite/Midget in various states of tune.

Intended usage	Late type filter head	Oil cooler	Oil thermostat	Sump mods.
Std/mild road	Yes	No	No	No
Medium road	Yes	Yes, 10 row	Yes	No
Fast road/mild comp.	Yes	Yes, 13 row	Yes	As required
All-out comp.	Yes	Yes, 16 row+	No	As required

Later type filter head for dispos-able filter canisters - plumbed with oil cooler line in this shot.

cheaper copies have been known to seriously degrade engine oil pressure because of their poor internal design.

Oil cooler

Having established the tem-perature range of the engine oil (by fitting a gauge) and finding it hotter than 230° F (110° C), the next priority is to fit an oil cooler. An oil cooler is a radiator that

Oil coolers come in all shapes and sizes - these are Serck units. Note the assortment of filter sandwich plates, thermostats and fittings. (courtesy Serck)

Later type filter head

A worthwhile modification that can be made whilst the engine is having an oil and filter change is the fitting of a filter head bracket that will take the later canister type of oil filter. The new bracket can be ob-tained inexpensively from Mini Spares Ltd. The old filter head bracket and case are unbolted from the block and discarded, then the new bracket is bolted to the block using a new gas-ket. The job is as simple as that. The canister type oil filter can now be fitted.

The main advantage in having a canister filter is that you can fill it with oil before fitting. This enables the engine oil pressure to be restored more quickly after an oil change. A canister filter is also a lot less messy than the element type to replace. Another alternative is to blank off the filter outlet on the block and fit a completely remote filter set-up; a modification covered in *Tuning BL's A-series Engine* by David Vizard.

A final note on filters. When you buy a filter I recommend you use a genuine Unipart item as

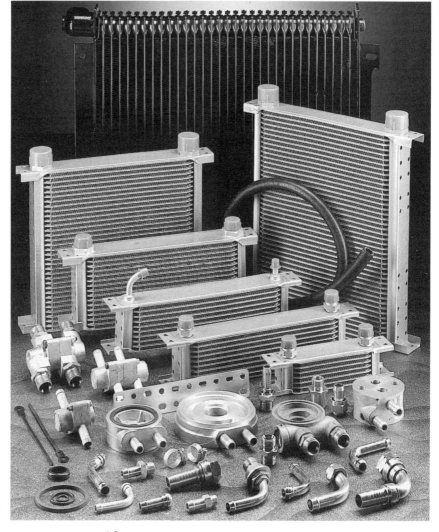

Above: One place to fit an oil cooler - this is a 16 row unit.

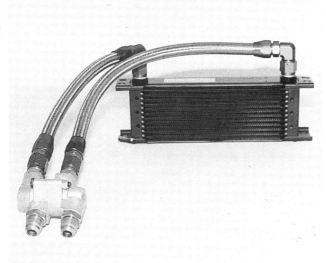

Right: Setrab oil cooler with Goodridge hose and thermostat before fitting to my Sprite.

radiator remains largely unaffected, despite what some people might tell you. This position also keeps the oil cooler reasonably well protected from flying stones and other road debris - remember a punctured oil cooler or pipe could result in sudden and complete loss of oil pressure..

To fit a cooler first remove the copper pipe connecting the engine block to the oil filter head and discard it. There are fittings in the kit to screw into the two outlets. From the fittings the oil pipe runs to the cooler unit. It does not matter which pipe runs to which end of the cooler as the oil flow in the cooler can be left to right or vice versa.

It's possible to use stainless steel braided hose and anodised alloy fittings manufactured by Goodridge in preference to the normal rubber hose supplied with a kit. The advantage lies in the stronger construction and obviously higher chafe resistance of the steel braiding. A bonus is that it also looks extremely business-like. I have also found that the normal pressure drop of 10psi (69kpa)or so on fitting a cooler with rubber pipes is practically eliminated when using Goodridge steel braided hose.

Oil thermostat

The only drawback with fitting an oil cooler is that in the winter it's possible to overcool the oil. To prevent this and to speed oil warm-up time, an oil thermostat will be required.

I have used Goodridge/Setrab oil thermostats for some years now and strongly recommend one for your road car. Be advised that some thermostats can be restrictive.

An oil thermostat is easy to fit to your oil cooler piping circuit. The two hoses leading to and from the oil cooler are cut in two, leaving you with four hose ends.

exchanges heat between the oil and the air. The flow of air through the matrix of the cooler unit cools the oil passing through it. The fitting of a cooler also increases the total oil capacity of the system by approximately the following amounts: 10 row - 0.23 Ltr, 13 row - 0.30 Ltr, 16 row - 0.37 Ltr; these figures only apply to the common long thin type of cooler and should capacity be an important consideration check the amount the cooler and its piping holds with the manufacturer.

Before fitting a cooler, the optimum size must be determined. This can be decided by reference to how much a reduction in temperature is needed. Ten rows is normal for a well tuned road car; thirteen for high performance road cars. For competition or very high performance road cars (120BHP +), 16 rows or larger may be necessary to keep the oil temperature around the 212° F (100° C) mark. To prevent over-cooling of the oil in cold weather and to assist initial warm-up an oil thermostat can be fitted to road cars.

Oil coolers can be bought in kit form, which usually comprises a cooler unit, all pipes and fittings and mounting brackets. The cooler needs positioning where it will receive good airflow. In my experience, bolting it in front of the radiator but behind the grille is near ideal. The cooler receives maximum airflow whilst the

Locate the union stub on the thermostat marked "Inlet" to which the hose leading from the filter head must be connected; the hose from the engine block should be connected to the union stub marked "Outlet". This allows for the oil to flow from the engine through the thermostat and back to the engine when the thermostat is in the closed position. The two remaining pipes from the thermostat lead to and from the cooler unit. When the oil reaches its operating temperature of around 172° F (78° C) the thermostat will open to divert the oil flow all the way to the cooler before returning to the engine.

Oil thermostats come in several sizes and I prefer the large unit. They are available from Goodridge and can have either push fit with hose clip connections or the tidier threaded hose fitting connections. Whichever installation you choose; before you drive off in your car check for oil leaks before and after allowing time for the oil to reach a working temperature. I have heard that the push fit and hose clamp connections can come off, though I never had any problems during the time I used this type of fitting. The completed job, if done correctly, should prevent damage to your engine through overheating. A lesson I learnt the hard way by virtue of a scuffed piston and blued piston pin bush (small end).

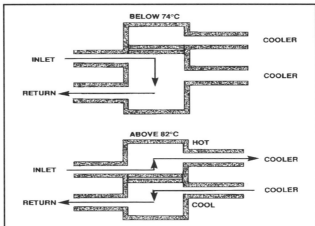

Above: Oil thermostat with Goodridge braided oil lines.

Left centre: This simple diagram shows the passage of the oil through an oil thermostat in open and closed positions. (drawing by Sharon Monroe)

Left: You may wish to fit an additional oil breather and catch tank (often mandatory for racing) as Geoff Hale has.

Peter May Eng. Ltd can supply you with an exchange baffled sump or baffle your existing sump. Finally, if you intend to rally your Sprite/Midget then it's possible to have a sump guard fabricated by any local metal worker, as did my friend Phil Bollen. However, remember that the sump guard should be designed to minimise the loss of airflow through the engine bay and around the sump.

Oil sump (oil pan)

There are modifications that can be made to the Sprite/Midget's sump and BL Special Tuning did make an extra deep sump and modified pick-up pipe for the Sprite/Midget at one time under part numbers "C-AJJ 3324" and "C-AJJ 3323" respectively. The only real advantage, I'm told by Rae Davis of Motobuild, is that the extra capacity allows for some oil consumption during a long race. If you do a lot of long distance racing you might try and get hold of this sump and pick-up, though it would probably be simpler to cut two sumps in half and then weld the deep sections together to provide the required increased depth: you'll also need to extend the pick-up pipe. If you find oil surge a problem then

12 EXHAUST SYSTEM

Introduction

Like the chapter on Weber conversion this chapter really applies to the A-series engine. However, as with inlet manifolds, Janspeed can supply an extractor manifold (header) and freeflow system for the 1500cc Midget which is the equivalent to the system I describe for the A-series engine.

There are numerous high performance exhaust manifolds (tube headers) and exhaust systems available for the A-series-engined Sprite/Midget. Large power and even economy gains can be made by switching to a high performance exhaust system. The higher tuned the engine the greater the power advantage becomes. A performance exhaust system need not be much more expensive or noisier than the standard exhaust.

Once more I recommend David Vizard's *Tuning BL's A-series Engine* which has an extensive chapter on exhaust systems. Rather than try to summarise or even plagiarize David's book I will recount my own views, experiences and preferences. You will find that usually I do agree with David Vizard, although my experiences are specifically with the Sprite/

A radical way of making sure your car's exhaust doesn't ground - Simon Page's turbo Frogeye Sprite.

Midget, my own car's engine producing a very impressive power figure as confirmed by chassis dynomometer testing.

Tubular manifolds (tube headers)

Most readers will have a preferred make of manifold (header), my own is Janspeed: they have an outstanding reputation backed up by huge amounts of dynomometer testing and race experience. For the Sprite/Midget the obvious modification for the exhaust system is to bin the cast manifold and replace it with the long centre branch tubular steel item. All aftermarket performance manifolds are made from tube steel and, for this reason, they're often known as tubular manifolds.

A change to a tubular manifold may create some problems in that it can produce more radiant heat than a standard cast manifold and. because of this, engine bay temperatures will rise: the A-series engine's intake and exhaust manifolds are on the same side of the engine so, in heavy traffic, the fuel in the carbs has a tendency to vaporize. Fuel vaporization causes rough idling and slow speed running until the car can be driven on the open road, allowing a good flow of air through the grille into the engine bay. I would like to put this problem into perspective by saying that it's only significant on very highly tuned engines on hot days, in traffic jams or during long periods of slow town driving. The problem of excess engine compartment heat can be drastically reduced by having louvres in the bonnet(hood) - see Chapter 17. You may be tempted to reduce excessive engine bay heating by wrapping the exhaust manifold with heat insulating tape: this will work, but there

is a downside. Insulation causes the pipes to run much hotter than would normally be the case, resulting in substantially reduced manifold life, especially with LCB types. It's certainly the case with Janspeed, and probably with other aftermarket exhaust manifold manufacturers too, that the use of insulation invalidates the manifold manufacturers warranty. For serious racers the need for regular manifold renewal may be an acceptable price to pay for the successful use of insulation.

LCB manifold (header)

The Long Centre Branch (LCB) manifold allows the exhaust gases to escape from the engine quickly and therefore reduce pumping losses, making the engine more efficient. When selecting a manifold check the bore size of the pipes. Also note how smooth the pipe bends are and how much attention has been paid to the joints.

The Janspeed 3-into-1 manifold (header) and collector box on my car.

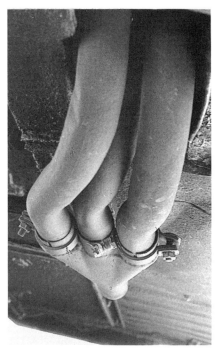

3-into-1 manifold (header)

The alternative to the LCB manifold is the 3- into-1. Oselli are able to supply a 3-into-1 manifold for the Sprite/Midget. For advice on manifold selection I refer you to the exhaust systems chapter in David Vizard's *Tuning BL's A-series Engine.*

Controlled vortex manifolds (headers)

A variation on LCB or 3-into-1 manifolds is the incorporation of a controlled vortex (CV) stub into the manifold. The subject is covered in depth in David Vizard's book as above.

The history of this type of manifold is quite short and can be briefly summarised as follows. The CV, or anti-reversion manifold, was developed by Janspeed in conjunction with David Vizard in 1981. At this time, Janspeed seriously marketed the CV manifold and it was popular amongst racers. However, the high cost of the manifold made it a less popular conversion for road cars. Also, the real benefits are not realised unless used on engines with large carburettor chokes and long period cams, these items being found only on the hottest of road cars. Because of the relatively very small demand, CV manifolds are made on a one-off basis and are quite expensive. Janspeed hold the British Patents for the CV manifold.

So what is the CV manifold and how does it work and what are the benefits? The CV manifold is different in that at the port end of the manifold it has small cones with a large space around them. From the outside this part of the manifold just looks slightly thicker. With an engine that is running a long duration cam there is a problem with exhaust gas back flowing through the port and into the combustion chamber because the valves are being held open longer than usual. The longer valve openings allow for high gas speed and optimum chamber filling at high rpm, but at low rpm can result in lower gas speed, reverse flow and power loss. The cones in the CV manifold hinder the back flow of exhaust gas: David Vizard has a full explanation, with diagrams, in his book. To quote Janspeed: "The controlled vortex manifolds are designed for competition cars running wild camshafts with high induction and exhaust gas speeds. The benefits of a controlled vortex manifold are that the engine will gain torque at the bottom to mid rpm range without loss of bhp at the top end. I would, however, stress that the engine will not gain brake horse power at the top end. As a by-product of increasing torque and hence lowering the usable rpm, you will also find that the car will become far more efficient fuel wise". David Vizard also says a great deal but the phrase "the extra low end torque would be instantly noticeable on the road" says it all.

I would say the CV manifold is very much underrated and feel that there are even benefits for full race cars because of the potential increase in torque. The extra power is very noticeable; my car ,when fitted with a CV manifold, had a noticeable and very pleasing surge in power from about 2700rpm to 4200rpm. The engine pulls much better across the whole rev range and is much smoother through gearchanges, particularly where the ratios are widest, both up and down the box. I also feel that changing from an LCB to the 3-into-1 CV manifold produces gains higher up the rev range. For my Sprite the gains have been made to a highly tuned 1312cc engine

which uses Kent Cams Megadyne 286 camshaft. In an engine using a longer duration cam such as the Megadyne 296 Race or 310 Full Race I imagine the advantages of the CV manifold would be even greater.

Ripspeed built a 1600cc A-series engine for a rallycross Mini using a CV manifold and said "it dropped the peak torque figure by 1000rpm" thereby making the engine much more driveable. It's important to remember, too, that it's torque that produces acceleration. The CV manifold will allow the use of a more radical (longer period/ increased overlap) camshaft in a road car with minimum loss of tractability.

There are further bonuses from using the Janspeed CV manifold apart from the exhaust benefits. A road car with a competition engine not only has to compromise in cam selection but also carburation calibration. On a Weber-engined car the choke (main venturi) will be smaller for maximum flexibility as required for town driving, but larger for maximum power output at high rpm. The most suitable choke size for out-and-out power will, in some cases, give a very flat engine response at 4000rpm yet a choke size 2mm smaller will be fine in all respects except for full power. As the power potential of the engine gets very high the gap between the desirable choke size and the practical choke size increases. I have found that with the CV manifold it is possible to go to the optimum choke size for full power and still retain good bottom end flexibility; in fact, more flexibility than when using small chokes with a conventional LCB manifold.

If you do opt for the Janspeed 3-into-1 manifold your car will probably be required for fitting of the exhaust manifold (header) as there isn't a pattern for this combination at the time of going to press. It is also neces-

One of the places where the car's body needs modification is where the manifold (header) downpipes exit the engine compartment. As the pipes sit right under the floorpan, the bare metal floor in my car has been known to melt passengers' footwear ...

sary during fitting to relieve one or two areas of bodywork to allow adequate clearance for the downpipes; Janspeed undertook this for me however, you'll find the necessary information in Chapter 17.

The exhaust system

The exhaust system is just as important as the manifold. In some cases more power, without loss of flexibility can be liberated by a good exhaust system than by a change of manifold however, it's always preferable to change both at the same time.

The system I run on my own heavily modified Sprite is the one David Vizard recommends in his book - the Mini Spares RC40, it will flow more cubic feet a minute (cfm) of exhaust gas than any other A-series system. Not only is it very efficient in gas flow and reduction

This is a full race RC40 exhaust system for the Mini.

I hung the single silencer box, via a short flexible strap, on a bracket that mounts on the rear bumper iron. The tailpipe will need shortening.

To suit the Sprite and Midget the front, cylindrical box of the RC40 is cut out and mild steel pipe welded in: this is a good place to fit one of the brackets to hang the system on. Alternatively, the RC40 rear silencer can be purchased as a unit.

in exhaust back pressure, it is also very efficient in silencing exhaust noise, more efficient than the next best system in cfm terms. For example on my Sprite, I have found it to be the quietest system I have ever used and I know that it also allows the best BHP production. Have no fear, it does still produce a healthy rorty exhaust note capable of turning heads! The only problem when using the RC40 system is that because it is designed to fit the Mini and Metro it does require some adaptation to fit the Sprite/ Midget. I originally hung my car's RC40 system with the silencer boxes in the original position Mini/Metro layout which, on the Sprite/Midget, gives a silencer box each side of the rear axle. You may be tempted to separate the boxes

and relocate them. However, Keith Dodd of Mini Spares Ltd informs me that the distance between the first and second box was determined by dyno testing and the spacing between boxes can be critical. An alternative is to use just the back silencer box which is available separately. I tried this on my second system and it proved much easier to fit and not much noisier. Fitting is simply a case of buying some large bore (sized to match the manifold and silencer) stainless steel tube and cutting it to a length that will fit from the manifold collector box pipe to the silencer system. A single straight pipe does the job. Depending which manifold is fitted you may find it necessary to heat and bend the pipe for ease of fitting. When using a LCB or 3-into-1

manifold, the pipe connection to the system may be quite close to the ground and therefore the preferred clamp to use at the join is a ring type as used on Volkswagen cars, as opposed to a conventional U-bracket. The system can be hung on universal flexible mounting brackets of the type that can be bought from your local exhaust stockist.
If you have lowered your Sprite/ Midget and use it on the road there can sometimes be a problem with clearance for the silencer box. I have never worried about this too much and take for granted the odd scrape on the box and, to date, I have never lost a box ... However, as a precaution, you may want to weld skid plates to the box and if you are stage or even special stage rallying your car this will be a necessity.
I have not mentioned any other exhaust system as in my experience the RC40 system is unrivalled. However, in his book, David Vizard does make comparisons between various systems as well as manifolds. The choice of combination is yours but the better informed you are the more effective your system is likely to be.

13 CLUTCH

Introduction

If your engine is producing big BHP you will almost certainly need to change the standard clutch for an uprated item. Motobuild or AP Racing can advise you on the best choice for your particular engine be it A-series or 1500. I've used a 6.5 inch (165mm) competition clutch disc in my A-series-engined car for years and I've only had one failure. As far as I know there is not a competition type clutch cover in 6.5 inches (165mm) available for the Sprite Midget A-series engined car

Modification options.

See the accompanying chart

Oversize clutch

If your car needs a really strong clutch it's possible to convert A-series-engined cars to a 7.5 inch (190.5mm) cover and disc which is available from AP or Peter May Eng. Ltd (clutch cover CP 2257/24, clutch disc CP 2257/11). To fit the larger clutch it's necessary to have the flywheel drilled for both dowels and bolts to the con-figuration of the larger clutch. It's also necessary to have the face of the flywheel machined flush to take the new clutch. I went to Peter May Eng. Ltd for this work to be done on my flywheel. At the same time as the flywheel was being modi-fied I had it balanced and lightened, as was the clutch

Intended usage	Roller clutch release	Comp. 6.5in (165mm) disc	Comp. 7.5in (190mm) plate & cover	Comp. 7.5in (190mm) sintered metal plate & cover
Mild road	Yes	Yes	No	No
Fast road/mild comp. 100bhp + at wheels	Yes	Yes	Desirable	No
All-out comp. 100bhp + at wheels	Yes, where possible	Yes, or sintered metal	Recomm-ended	Yes, if bhp very high

Above: Roller clutch release bearing by Peter May Eng. Ltd.

Left: Shiny area is where I've ground metal away to clear 7.5 inch (290mm) clutch.

really the best people to advise you on selection.

Conclusion

You should be aware that a competition clutch will be more expensive, heavier to operate and less smooth in power transi-tion, so don't fit one unless you really need to.

14 GEARBOX (TRANSMISSION)

Introduction

This chapter covers a number of gearbox modifications ranging from simple lever shortening to fitting a Toyota 5-speed unit. Your choice of modifications will largely depend on how you use your car, although, if competition is a consideration, any class regulations will also dictate what can be done.

Basically gearboxes are modified to match engine characteristics to intended use by changing the gear ratios of some or all of the gears. This aim can be achieved in one of two ways: fitting replacement gearsets in the existing gearbox casing or by swopping the entire gearbox for another unit with more appropriate characteristics.

Shorter gearshift lever

The simplest and cheapest modification in the gear changing department is to shorten the gearshift lever. I have found the standard lever is much too long, even for my relatively short arms. Shortening the lever is one way of improving Sprite/Midget cockpit ergonomics: I find a short lever aids quick and smooth gear changes. How much you shorten will depend, of course, on your seat position, arm reach, etc., but I find 1 inch to 1.5 inches (25.4-38mm) is ideal. However, I know that some racers use a stick that is a lot shorter than this.

You can approach the shortening in one of two ways. Either cut the lever in two, cut out the length you require and then weld it back together , or cut the lever to the required height and re-thread the 'new' top of the stick. The choice is immaterial and dictated only by the tools and equipment at your disposal. Once done, the gearshift lever can be refitted in a few moments and you can enjoy shifting those cogs faster!

Complete straight cut, close ratio gear set-up for the Sprite/Midget. Noisy but efficient!

80

New ratios & straight cut gears

If a gear ratio change is contemplated then only a limited number of choices exist. You can install a set of close ratio straight cut gears (as close ratio gears are invariably used for competition they are nearly always cut straight, and I know of no close ratio helical cut gears that can be used in the Sprite/Midget gearbox). Alternatively, if a reader has an unusual application where wider ratios would be more useful, gearsets from the Morris Minor will fit A-series-engined Sprite/Midget gearbox (transmission). However, for a racer or high performance road car it will be the close ratios that are required.

A close ratio gear kit is not cheap at all, but is worth the investment if you're serious about performance. As the fitting of the close ratio gears involves rebuilding the gearbox it's obviously worth spending the extra money and fully reconditioning the gearbox at the same time. My personal experience is that you'll only get what you pay for if you're getting someone else to do the work and your local gearbox so-called 'specialist' might not actually do that good a job. In the past I've had a gearbox reconditioned and re-installed it in my car only to discover that, although it no longer whined, it still jumped out of gear! Bearing this in mind I recommend that you go to a reputable builder with real experience of the Sprite/Midget box. My personal recommendation for readers in the UK is reknowned Austin Healey expert, Dave Hardy, who I went to for my rebuilt gearbox as do many racers. Dave Hardy, Peter May Eng. and Motobuild can all supply gearbox parts.

To give an idea of the difference between ratios refer to the nearby accompanying table for comparison. Should you wish to work out the mph potential for each ratio just use the simple formula given in Chapter 15 (Drivetrain).

Conversion to 5-speed gearbox

The alternative to fitting the straight cut close ratio gear kits is to go for the popular five-speed conversion. This modification involves replacing the gearbox, bellhousing and other parts with a Toyota box. The kit itself is quite well known now and comes from a company called Dellow Automotive in Australia. Originally available from Rooster Racing it is now retailed by Minor Mania Ltd (in the UK.) who, as their name

Toyota's 5-speed gearbox (transmission) squeezed into Simon Page's 'Frogeye' Sprite - note metal braided hose clutch hydraulic liine.

Right: Another view of the Toyota box installed in Simon's turbo Frogeye.

Below: Minor Mania supplies Toyota 5-speed conversion, here mounted on a display stand.

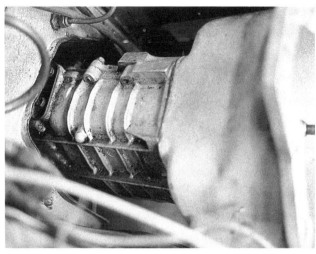

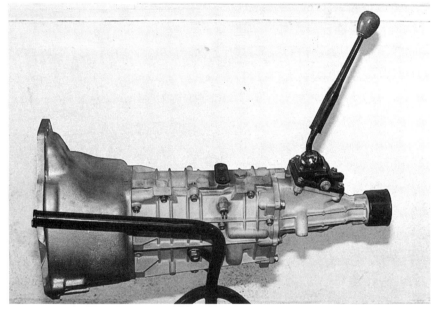

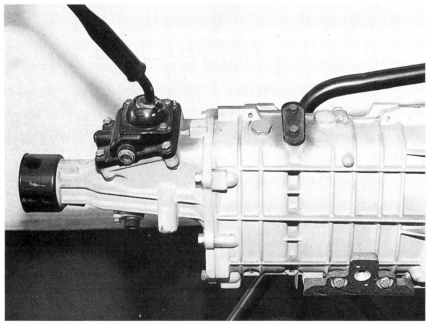

suggests, are mainly Morris Minor experts. Many people have successfully fitted the kit both to Minors and of course Sprites and Midgets.

Fitting to the Sprite/Midget is only applicable to A-series-engined cars and does involve a slightly different approach to fitting than to the Minor. I have not personally fitted the kit but I understand it is quite straightforward if you follow the instructions supplied. The principle advantage of the conversion is that not only do you get the extra overdrive ratio fifth gear, but also gain synchromesh on first gear. Another advantage of the Toyota box is that it very strong and can easily handle the extra torque generated by even turbocharged engine conversions.

The Toyota ratios are fairly similar to those of the Sprite/Midget box, though should you require a set of straight cut close ratio gears for this box they are available through Toyota Sport GB and, no doubt equivalent organizations worldwide. At the time of going to press gear sets available by special order only from Japan so allow several months for delivery.

Gear ratios

Gear ratios for various Sprite/Midget and Toyota gearboxes are detailed in the accompanying chart.

Midget 1500 overdrive conversion

For 1500cc-engined cars there is one difficult, but very worthwhile, mod which is to replace the standard gearbox with the Triumph overdrive gearbox. I've not been able to talk to anyone

Left Speedo drive on Toyota 'box is on opposite side to the Sprite/Midget unit.

	1st	2nd	3rd	4th	5th
Frogeye Sprite	3.627	2.374	1.412	1.00	-
Sprite Midget 1275	3.2	1.916	1.357	1.00	-
Sprite Midget special tuning close ratio	2.573	1.722	1.255	1.00	-
Spitfire 1500	3.50	2.16	1.433	1.00	-
Midget 1500	3.4118	2.119	1.433	1.00	-
Midget 1500 close ratio	2.65	1.76	1.25	1.00	-
Toyota Celica 2T	3.587	2.022	1.384	1.00	0.861

who has actually done this conversion, but did hear that a few 1500cc Midgets have had this box and unit successfully fitted.

Gearbox (transmission)

lubricants

For road and competition use I strongly recommend the use of synthetic oils and I have found Mobil products work well: 5/50 Mobil One for non-1500cc gearboxes and SAE Mobil gear oil for 1500cc cars. Sprite/ Midget gearbox capacities are given in workshop manuals and handbooks, whilst the capacity for the Toyota box is 2.8 pints (1.5 litres).

15 DRIVETRAIN

Introduction

Following the gearbox in the power path to the back wheels are the propshaft, crownwheel and pinion, differential and half shafts (driveshafts). For the purposes of this book the foregoing components are defined as the 'drivetrain' although the term would normally be taken to include the gearbox (transmission) and clutch. The drivetrain can be strengthened and, of course, the crownwheel and pinion offers the possibility of a final drive ratio change. Lastly, a limited slip differential can improve traction hugely.

Modification options

The accompanying chart shows which modifications are desirable in relation to intended usage.

Propshaft balancing

With the aid of a workshop manual you'll find removal of the propshaft easy. Balancing the propshaft may sound like a luxury but experience has strongly indicated that racing or use of a low final drive ratio will quickly bring to light any propshaft imbalance. Since balancing is a specialist job I took my car's propshaft to a specialist company for not only balancing but for a full overhaul also. The company was Reco-Prop who specialise in propshaft balancing and overhaul for virtually all purposes, including classics and racing cars.

My car's propshaft showed excessive wear and one of the UJs showed signs of seizing, although in use nothing felt amiss ... The UJs were removed and new cups and bearings fitted. Rust is removed from the shaft before balancing and, once balanced, the shaft is

Intended usage	Balance propshaft	Limited slip diff.	Competition halfshafts
Std/mild road	Yes	Desirable	No
Fast road	Yes	Very desirable	Only for high output engines
Competition	Yes	If class regs. permit	Yes

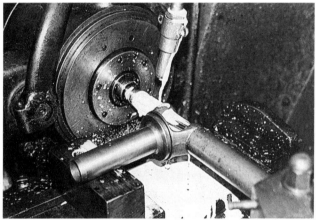

Top left: My car's propellor shaft (driveshaft) being dynamically balanced at Reco Prop. (courtesy Reco Prop)

Top right: Propshaft completely dismantled. (courtesy Reco Prop)

Centre right: Propshaft yoke being reamed. (courtesy Reco Prop)

Left: Bearing cup retaining clips being fitted to conclude UJ rebuild. (courtesy Reco Prop)

even given a fresh coat of paint. Refitting the shaft is straightforward but make sure you use fresh self-locking nuts and bolts.

If you are converting your car to the Toyota 5 speed gearbox you will need to modify the propshaft by using the front yoke and part of the shaft from a Toyota. However. I understand it is simpler to use the whole Toyota shaft and fit the rear Sprite/Midget rear yoke to it.

Left: Standard differential unit in early type carrier.

Differential, crownwheel and pinion

Moving on down the driveline we come to the differential, crownwheel and pinion. For ease of understanding it is best to view this group of components as two separate assemblies: 1) the crownwheel and pinion which turn the drive through 90° and provide a drive ratio between pinion and crownwheel, and 2) the differential which distributes power to the rear wheel with the best grip.

One of the most important considerations when it comes to the back axle is the choice of a final drive ratio which should suit the vehicle's intended use. Once again, you'll need to consider carefully what is required. Your choice will also be influenced by the gearbox ratios used, be they standard, close ratio or Toyota standard 5-speed gears or possibly even close ratio Toyota 5-speed. There are three commonly available final drive ratios for the Sprite/Midget, these being: 3.727, 3.9 and 4.222. Lesser known and much lower ratios

are also available from the parts bins of the Morris quarter-ton van - 4.555, A35 van - 4.875, and the Morris GPO van - 5.375. If these ratios are unavailable it is always possible to have a set specially cut by an expert gear cutter like Schofield & Samson Ltd. Diff carriers come in early or late type and not all ratios are interchangeable as this simple guide chart illustrates.

Ratio	No. of teeth	Late or early diff.*
3.727	11/41	Fits late
3.9	10/39	Fits late
4.222	9/38	Fits late
4.8	8/39	Only fits early
5.375	8/43	Only fits early

Cars from H-AN7-24732 and G-AN2-16184 onwards will only take late type diff ratios. Late type diff assemblies can be identified as having the oil filler plug in the diff housing as opposed to the axle case.

It's possible to calculate the potential speed of the car with different gearings by using differential and gear ratios to arrive at the correct speed for any given engine speed. Here is the simple formula to calculate it -

$$\frac{60,000}{Dr \text{ \& } WRPM} = mph \text{ in top gear}$$

("Dr" = diff ratio, "WRPM" = wheel revs per mile)

Calculate miles per hour in intermediate gears using this formula -

$$\frac{Top \text{ gear mph per 1000 rpm}}{gear \text{ ratio}}$$

To get the wheel revs per mile figure you will need to contact your local tyre dealer or the tyre manufacturer. However, the following are examples of some approximate wrpm for a selection of tyres:

145 x 13 = 936wrpm

155 x 13 = 914wrpm

175 x 13 = 908wrpm

Having obtained the necessary values it is now a simple matter to finish the speed calculation as follows -

Assuming our test car has a 3.9 diff on 145 x 13 tyres we can work out that 60,000 divided by 3.9 x 936 = 16.44mph per thousand engine rpm in top gear. We want the figure for, say, 5000rpm in top gear, so it's a simple case of multiplying our 1000rpm figure by five, ie 5 x 16.44mph = 82mph. To work out speeds in intermediate gears, simply divide the top gear speed at 1000rpm by the relevant intermediate gear ratio. For example, using the 16.44mph top gear at 1000rpm

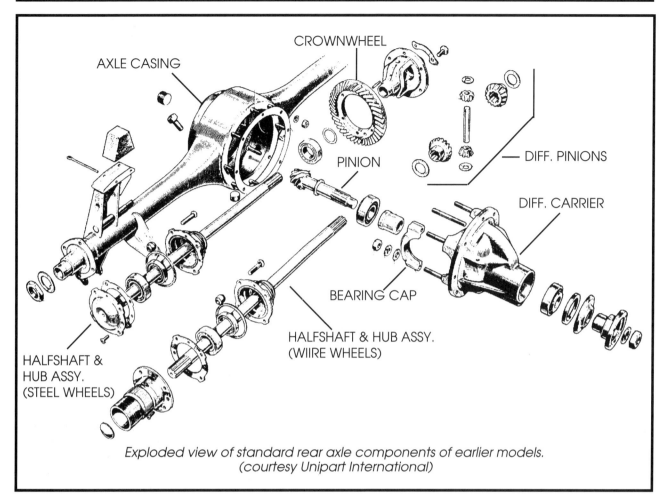

Exploded view of standard rear axle components of earlier models.
(courtesy Unipart International)

Labels on figure:
AXLE CASING
CROWNWHEEL
DIFF. PINIONS
DIFF. CARRIER
PINION
BEARING CAP
HALFSHAFT & HUB ASSY. (WIIRE WHEELS)
HALFSHAFT & HUB ASSY. (STEEL WHEELS)

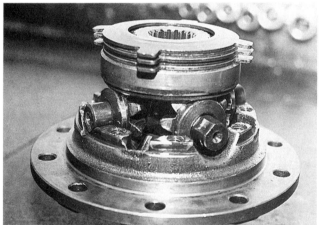

Clutch plate type LSD, less cover - this is a Jaguar unit.

Quaife Torsen differential in early type carrier with 3.9 ratio crownwheel and pinion.

figure divided by the standard third gear ratio of 1.412:1 (16.44 divided by 1.412 = 11.64mph per 1000rpm) we get the 1000rpm speed of 11.64mph for third gear. Multiply this figure appropriately to get the car's speed at any engine speed: *ie*

5 x 11.64 = 58mph (at 5000rpm).

Limited slip differentials

Competition type diffs, which replace the standard diff unit, can be of the limited slip or Torsen automatic torque biasing

type. Either type of diff is designed to improve traction by feeding power to both wheels at all times, the wheel with best grip getting the most. The benefits can be felt not only during race type standing starts, but also when attempting to put maximum power down hard at the exit of a corner, especially in the wet.

The most common type of limited slip diff (LSD) is the clutch plate type where the friction of the clutch plates ensures that drive is never totally lost to either wheel. Motobuild Ltd retail this type of diff. The alternative to the conventional LSD is the Torsen type automatic torque biasing diff which employs helical gears and which, when one wheel spins, locks and transmit power equally across the diff. Quaife manufacture and retail the Torsen principle diff and it is available direct from them in the UK and in the United States from retailers such as Victoria British Ltd.

In use each diff will provide a substantial improvement to the handling of the car, whether in day-to-day driving (especially in the wet) or competition work. I understand from some racers that the Torsen Quaife diff is much more user friendly than the clutch plate type LSD and less likely to let the car snake when undertaking a racing start.

Having decided to fit a competition diff and made your choice of diff type it is time to get it fitted. You can, of course, do the job yourself but it may be worth letting the diff manufacturer do the job for you, which in my case was R T Quaife Eng. They prefer diffs that are going to be fitted with their Torsen diff to be delivered complete rather than in a stripped down state. The reason for this is that it is simpler to swap the parts over when rebuilding the diff.

Changing rear axle ('diff') ratios

On the face of it changing the final drive 'diff' ratio should be straightforward but, in practice, this may not be the case be-

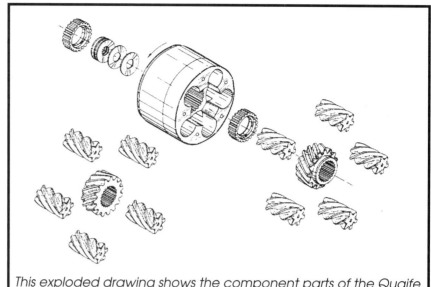

This exploded drawing shows the component parts of the Quaife differential, clearly illustrating its gear design. (courtesy Quaife)

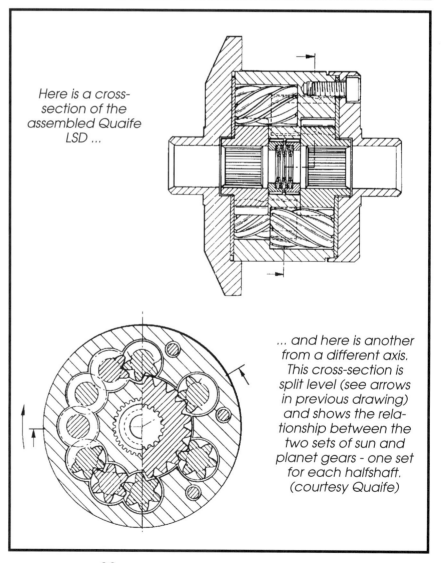

Here is a cross-section of the assembled Quaife LSD ...

... and here is another from a different axis. This cross-section is split level (see arrows in previous drawing) and shows the relationship between the two sets of sun and planet gears - one set for each halfshaft. (courtesy Quaife)

Standard (with carrier bearings) and Quaife diffs side-by-side.

Motobuild-supplied LSD for Sprite/Midget.

cause, as mentioned earlier, not all carriers and casings accept all ratios. It may not be apparent until the diff is stripped whether the new ratios are compatible; if they are different you'll find that both spacers and thrust washers for the pinion will need to be machined to fit or new parts will need to be turned from steel bar.

Once the pinion has been shimmed and fitted with new bearings and oil seal, the crownwheel and diff can be offered up to the carrier with new bearings; however, the second major problem may be experienced at this stage. The crownwheel and diff may be too large for the carrier. If so, the only way to get the non-standard crownwheel to fit is to use a different, later carrier, or machine the existing carrier. From experience I advise that if you are using a Quaife diff with 3.9, 3.7, or 4.2 ratios, you use a later carrier.

Although it is not deemed necessary to run (break in) the

Competition halfshaft complete with Peter May's hand!

diff, I certainly recommend treating it gently for the first few miles and carrying out a precautionary 500 mile (800km) first oil change. I strongly recommend the use of the Mobil Synthetic gear oil Mobilube SHC (SAE 75W-90); it's expensive but, I believe, worth it.

Competition halfshafts

If you are using your car for competition it's possible to get uprated halfshafts (Rover part number "C-BTA-939" for wire wheels and "C-BTA-940" for normal wheels). If you are unable to obtain competition halfshafts using these numbers it's possible to have shafts specially made by R T Quaife Engineering for wire wheel cars and Peter May Eng. can supply competition shafts for steel or alloy wheeled cars. Motobuild can also supply competition halfshafts. My experience is that only cars with over a hundred brake horsepower at the wheels and on treaded tyres need competition halfshafts, but reduce this figure to 80bhp at the wheels if you are using slick racing tyres.

16 INSTRUMENTS & ELECTRICAL COMPONENTS

Introduction

Whether using your car for road or track there are several things that can be done to improve instrumentation, so enabling an eye to be kept on what is happening. This should help avoid expensive engine 'melt downs' and other terminal failures for all but the most inattentive. If your engine is modified to any degree keep an eye on the temperature until you know the cooling system can hold its own under all conditions.

Note that a number of electrical modifications appear in other chapters.

Oil temperature gauge

High engine temperatures can be reflected by oil as well as water temperatures. It follows then that an indicated high oil temperature is a good clue to imminent engine-damaging overheating. Even if you have fitted an oil cooler and perhaps a thermostat, too, your engine can still overheat: for instance, the oil thermostat could stick in the closed position, although this is unusual. More likely, during an intensive period of rolling road tuning where the engine is working hard under load, you will discover the limits of your engine's oil cooling system! The fitting of an oil temperature gauge is always a wise precaution for cars with high performance engines. Gauges can be operated by two types of sensor. One fits into an oil line but I'm not particularly keen on this type because I believe the oil is always likely to be cooler in the line than in the sump. For that reason I have always used the second, and much more common type, which is a sensor fitted in the sump (oil pan). Normally this type can only be fitted with the oil drained and the sump removed. (As a point of interest I understand that it is possible to fit a sensor directly into the sump plug, though this is something I've not tried myself). Therefore, the most economic way to do the job is to wait until the next service interval oil and filter change (especially if, like

Sensor for oil temperature gauge.

This is where the oil temperature sensor fits in my car's sump (oil pan) but it would have been better placed nearer the drain plug for ease of removal.

sump. Install the sensor and, using a new gasket, refit the sump, then refill the engine with oil. Check for leaks before and after the engine has warmed up.

Now that you have an oil temperature gauge you will observe that the engine can take quite a time to reach operating temperatures. If no indication is seen on the gauge, re-check the installation for slip-ups. With

In my car's dash, oil gauges have prominence and petrol and water gauges sit in a small pod under the dash.

me, you use Mobil One which is too expensive to waste). The parts required to plumb in the gauge should all be contained in one kit. The only exception may be the sump gasket and a supplementary instrument pod. Fit the gauge and its mounting pod in the desired location. If you are short of ideas I suggest fitting below the existing dash but check pod to gearlever clearance in first and top gear positions. I favour the capillary type gauge and with this type it's necessary to pass the sensor and capillary tubing through the engine bulkhead before fitting to the sump. An addi-

tional hole can be drilled but check to see if an existing grommeted hole exists that is usable. When the sensor is dangling in the engine bay check clearance to the chassis leg. Be sure to mark a sensor location that allows adequate room for the sensor (in other words check its protrusion). Next remove the sump and drill the hole in the required position. The sensor mount must now be brazed into the hole. After studiously cleaning all metal swarf from the sump, fill with Paraffin (Kerosene) and check there are no leaks. If everything is okay, drain and clean up the

the newly installed gauge you will readily gain experience of the temperature your engine is likely to run at, be it around town, the motorway (freeway) or racetrack. Use this experience to determine if your engine requires a larger, or maybe even smaller, oil cooler.

Oil pressure warning light

Still on the subject of oil, your Sprite/Midget should have a low oil pressure warning light in the standard instrumentation. This is normally a small orange

Simon Page's car's dash is neat and functional and includes turbo boost gauges. Note larger low oil pressure warning light and genuine Pool number 8 ball gearlever knob!

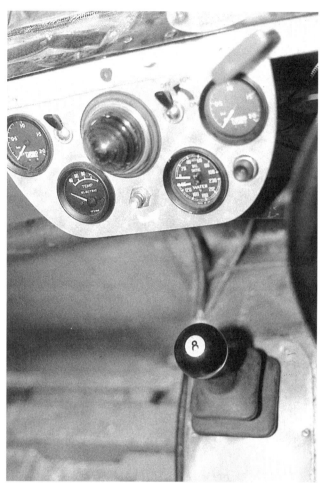

light set in the speedometer or tachometer. If your car has a non-standard speedometer, tachometer or oil pressure gauge this light may have been disconnected or relocated. Whatever the situation a worthwhile modification can be made here.

An oil light is operated by an oil pressure switch installed in the block, often as part of the unions for the pressure gauge. Though available in different settings these usually trip at about 5psi (35kpa) pressure. As a means of indicating some oil pressure has been achieved this is fine but next to useless if a sudden loss of engine oil pressure occurs at high engine speed as, with only 5 pounds or less of oil pressure, you may have the beginnings of a lot of engine damage. To help avoid this install a high pressure oil switch which will trip at the

higher and more useful pressure of around 20-25psi (138-173kpa). The high pressure switch kit may or may not come complete but in most instances it is simply a case of off with the old switch and on with the new.

You can, of course, as many racers do, fit a larger and more obvious warning light to the dash panel.

Water temperature sensor

The car's existing water temperature gauge will give you a reasonable indication of the water temperature. Under many circumstances higher than normal water temperatures may be experienced when driving in stop/start traffic, but you should be able to resolve any cooling problems or shortcomings by

reference to the cooling chapter. However, if you don't watch the gauge like a hawk, the first indication that a problem exists may be an embarrassing cloud of steam while waiting to show the car alongside a clean pair of wheels. Alternatively, a hose may burst and you may not be aware of this until excessive engine heat has taken its toll.

The solution is to fit a simple temperature sensing switch which is available from Kenlowe. This can be used to activate a dashboard mounted idiot light when the coolant temperature reaches an adjustable, pre-determined level. As an alternative, or in addition, a warning buzzer can also be wired to be activated simultaneously.

Tachometer

On high performance cars one of the most important instruments is the tachometer and, if you are running a highly tuned engine, you might replace the standard item with a more accurate instrument. I recommend this as the standard tachometer can often be inaccurate at 6500rpm and beyond.

If you are after the ultimate in aftermarket tachometers then take a look at the range from Stack. Not only are these highly accurate instruments but there is a wide choice of dials to suit your application. In addition, not only can you have a tachometer tell tale, but also an action replay facility of up to 5 minutes. Better still is a longer performance analysis with up to 25 minutes' recall on a printout. All aftermarket tachometers come with comprehensive fitting instructions and are simple to fit. However, you may need to fit dash mounted warning lights to replace those previously situated in the face of the original tachometer.

Stack tachos are available in a range of faces

Stack tachos are available with full printout facility but are expensive - I'm still saving up for mine.

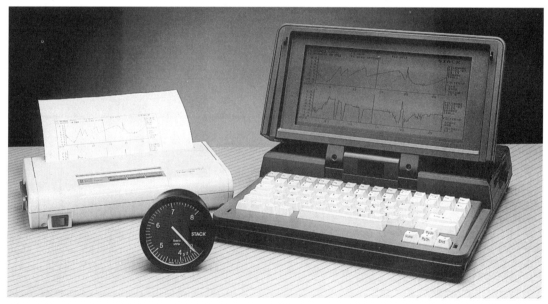

Two-speed windscreen (windshield) wiper conversion

For anyone wishing to convert their Sprite/Midget from single speed to two-speed wipers there is a simple and cost effective means available. The conversion can be made either by using a new or second-hand wiper motor.

I used an Austin Maxi wiper motor, but there is no reason why a motor from any of the other BMC/BL models can't be used; providing, of course, that it is the same basic type as the Sprite/Midget motor. As the wiper motor has a running current of only 3.1amps the new wire need only be of 0.33mm thickness or more; the new wire can be taped to the existing wiring loom. A three-way switch will be needed to complete the conversion. To match the existing dash layout I used a Sprite/Midget 3-way light switch to replace the old 2-way wiper switch. Depending on the year of your car you may adopt a different switch to match the existing switch gear. Some

electrical wire and connectors are also required for the conversion.

Before the new motor can be fitted the old one must be removed. First disconnect the wiring block connector at the motor and then unfasten the motor brackets. Remove the motor drive cover to expose the drive pinion and cable. The drive cable can now be pulled off the pinion crank then the motor can be removed from the car.

At this point it may be worth checking to see how freely the wiper wheelboxes turn inde-

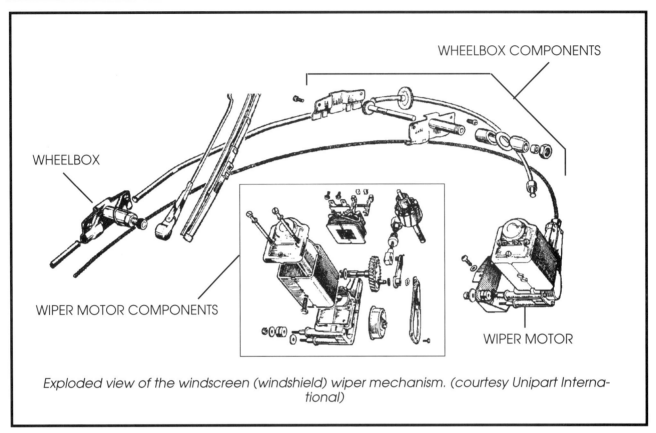

Exploded view of the windscreen (windshield) wiper mechanism. (courtesy Unipart International)

WHEELBOX COMPONENTS

WHEELBOX

WIPER MOTOR COMPONENTS

WIPER MOTOR

Right: Wiper motor with cover removed - large pinion has degree of sweep stamped on it: 110° in this case.

pendently of the motor by pulling the wiper cable to and fro. If there is a great deal of resistance it is most likely to be due to excessive friction in the wheelboxes. If this is the case remove the boxes and drill a small hole in the body of each wheelbox. Next, through this hole squirt a silicone-based lubricant such as WD40. Turn the wiper blade shaft in the wheelbox and repeatedly squirt the lubricant into the unit until it frees off. The wheelboxes should now be refitted and you'll find that they provide trouble-free service at considerably less cost than replacement items.

Put the two-speed wiper motor alongside the single speed motor and remove the drive motor cover. Turn each motor the other way and release the circlip from the centre of the pinion shaft. The pinion on

eachmotor can now be removed.

By swopping over the two drive pinions the two-speed motor now has the correct sweep stroke for the Sprite/Midget as it has been fitted with the Sprite/Midget drive pinion. Reassembly is simply a reversal of the strip down.

Refit the converted motor and refit the electrical block connector. Run an extra wire to the spare spade terminal on the two-speed motor or, if you prefer, fit a new connector block and use it to connect the new wire. Wire up the new 3-way switch to incorporate the extra wire. The wiring is the most complicated part of the conversion and the type of switch you use will dictate the manner of connection. You may find it helpful to use a circuit tester to sort out any wiring problems. Having done all this you now have one of the very few two-speed wiper Sprite/Midgets on the road; I believe mine was the very first.

Lighting

You can easily fit high output quartz halogen headlamps in place of the standard units but if you do this, or fit high output driving lamps, you may need to switch the new lights via a relay because the electrical load is too high for dashboard switches. Consult the manufacturer or supplier of the lights you are intending to fit and follow their recommendations.

Conclusion

As you can see there are quite a few things to consider when altering instrumentation and I have deliberately not described any set layout as your own needs will dictate your requirements and preferences.

17 BODY

Introduction

As you have read about various modifications you will have been referred to this chapter a few times. Here, you'll find several bodywork modifications unique to the Sprite/Midget and also some general advice.

Wheelarches

Front wheelarches need no introduction and any flare you put on them will simply be big enough to accommodate your chosen width of wheel and tyre combination at full lock and full bump. I suggest that the following method will produce the neatest flared arch. Cut the existing arch with tin snips at regular intervals, each cut being at 90° to its section of wheelarch, then peel out the sections to the amount of flare you require. The segments should then be dressed with a dolly and hammer to the required shape. Carefully tack weld the segments and then dress again with the hammer and dolly as required. Finish off the arch using a light skim of body filler or lead loading. I actually took my car to Carcraft in Ipswich for this work to be done; they are MG specialists and have looked after

The front arch on my car's new wing being flared by Carcraft. (courtesy Carcraft)

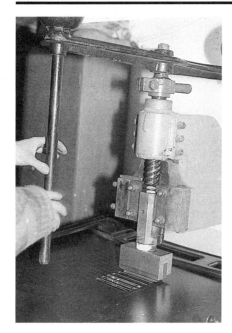

Top left: All louvres are hand punched on a fly press at Kool Louvre Ltd.

Left: Robin Pocock proudly displays finished bonnet (hood) for my car.

Below: the freshly painted louvred bonnet on my car - louvres are sited for maximum hot air escape in exhaust manifold area. Note adhesive license plate for neatness.

the bodywork on my car since I moved into the area.

Rear wheelarches on the Sprite/Midget can be either square or round. Round arches can be flared like the front arches and need no further mention. Square arches, on the other hand, are quite hard to flair and Carcraft chose to raise the arch height on my car so as to retain the original look but allow the use of a wider tyre/wheel combination. This can be a difficult job and perhaps one best done while having both inner and outer wings renovated which was what happened in my case. If you choose this type of flair check for wheel clearance before completing the job by jacking up the axle from one side and then the other, remembering that the axle will probably move from side to side during hard cornering. A final point is to check the dishing (or offset) of the wheels you intend to use as this can affect arch clearance more than simply going up to a larger tyre size.

The only company I know who makes fibreglass wheelarch flares specifically for Sprite/Midget is USA based Sports and Classics who manufacture rear arches in good quality fibreglass

for 1962 and later models.

Bonnet (hood) louvres (vents)

As I mentioned in earlier chapters, engine bay temperatures can become a problem in hot weather. The only solution is to let some of the hot air out through the bonnet and this is done by the use of louvres. Louvres have been used on production cars as diverse as the E-type Jaguar and the Sierra Cosworth. It's possible to go for the traditional punched metal look or the modern fibreglass look: the choice is yours.

To fit Cosworth louvres it is necessary to fit fibreglass inserts into holes cut in the bonnet and this can be very tricky to accomplish on a steel bonnet but is easier with fibreglass bonnets

and one piece fronts commonly fitted to Frogeye Sprites and racing Sprites and Midgets. Fitting louvres to a fibreglass bonnet can be achieved by

This fibreglass louvre panel (vents need to be cut) is modelled on the Cosworth Sierra item but could easily be used for Sprite/ Midget.

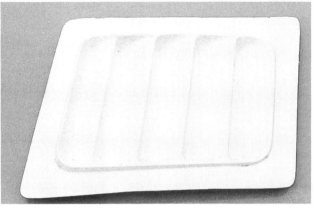

amateurish and attract a lot of adverse comment (like my original modified bonnet did). An alternative is to cut a hole and fibreglass-in a suitable pre-made bulge of your own design and which can have been formed on any suitable ball or curved object you choose. By far the neatest option is to take the bonnet to your local bodyshop and let them do the job professionally with a panel hammer and dolly.

'glassing-in', pop riveting or securing by self-tapping screws. For steel or aluminium bonnets real louvring can only be done by a special tool in a machine press. One company I know of that can do this is Kool Louvre in Aylesbury, England. Kool Louvre is, in fact, Robert Pocock and I took a new Ron Hopkinson-supplied bonnet down to his workshop to have louvres punched. Kool Louvre can punch louvres from 1 inch up to 5 inches in width and there is no limit to how many - other than the strength of the bonnet! You tell Robert the positioning, number and size of louvres: he does the rest. I settled on a double row over the exhaust manifold towards the rear edge of the bonnet. (Try to avoid positioning the louvres within 12 to 18 inches (300 to 460mm) of the windscreen. The position I chose allows for a really good escape of hot air as the area beneath is a heat trap. You may, of course, wish to experiment and find a good low pressure area in the air steam or try the middle of the bonnet. Circuit race cars, hillclimbers and sprinters may prefer a great many more louvres than I chose and this is not a problem. I particularly like the cut louvres as aside from being functional they add to the styling of the

Right: Necessary relief of inner wing to give clearance for a DCOE carburettor using 39mm rams and K&N filter.

car and produce that authentic sixties look.

Throttle linkage clearance (Weber DCOE)

If you have fitted a Weber and a Janspeed throttle linkage you may be looking for this short paragraph. You have two choices; either you modify the linkage (as Carcraft did for my car) or you'll need a bonnet (hood) bulge to prevent the linkage jamming against the underside of the bonnet and this bulge can be patiently beaten out with a large ball pein hammer but may look

Tubular exhaust manifold clearance

If you're using a tubular exhaust manifold (tube header), you may find (certainly with the Janspeed 3-into-1 manifold) that some extra clearance is required at the 90° bend and the bottom of the pipes. When Janspeed manufactured and fitted my CV 3-into-1 manifold they made the necessary relief for the manifold to fit. If you are fitting an performance exhaust manifold yourself you may need to provide the relief in order for the manifold to fit. This will require cutting back the metal to clear the downpipe and then, if required, welding of the seam.

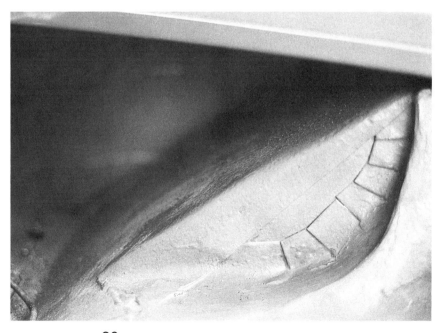

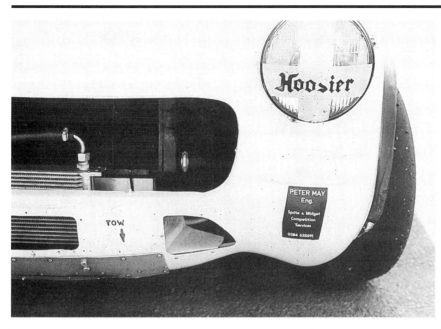

Karl Barras' race car has tidy air ducting for front brakes, also cut-out in front panel to increase air flow to low mounted (minimal obstruction of radiator) oil cooler.

Carburettor, air filter and ram clearance

Moving from exhaust considerations to induction, I found that on my car the long(ish) rams I use for maximum engine flexibility as well as horsepower required a relief in the inner wing (fender) to allow room for a suitably sized air filter to accommodate them. When later I substituted Induction Technology full radius (FR) rams, the width became a consideration as well. As with the throttle linkage clearance problem I originally did the job myself with an extremely large hammer and then had the job done properly at a later date by a professional bodyshop.
Aside from the relief of the inner wing, a very large air filter may also require some minimal relief at the bonnet edge.

Aluminium and fibreglass panels

You may, unlike myself, have a healthy bank account that will run to a lot of aluminium panels. The whole point of using aluminium is that it is light and therefore of use to the racer. But, there is no reason why you can't have a lightweight road car. Motobuild list a whole range of aluminium panels in

Paul Rodman's 1500cc Midget has neat one-piece front.

Full body conversions

Other modifications for the Sprite/Midget are full body kits such as the Arkley and Lenham which are covered in Lindsay Porter's *Sprite/Midget Purchase and DIY Restoration* book. Of the two, the Arkley conversion is no longer available and I have heard little of the Lenham.

A third and even rarer conversion is the Speedwell conversion. Speedwell, before their demise, made numerous tuning parts for the Sprite/Midget, but perhaps the most interesting parts they made were the bodywork conversions and bonnets. Just before this book was due to go to press I heard from Richard E. Rooks in the United States who has researched the Speedwell story in some depth; I had hoped to include the full story in this book but limitations on space pre-

their catalogue and include the following: front nose skin (between wings), boot lid skin, door pillar outer skin, and many others. For some applications, like racing, you may wish to fabricate the parts yourself. Front spoilers are also available from Motobuild or Sports and Classics in the USA but, to my knowledge, only in fibreglass. Another modification that is frequently made to the Sprite/Midget is, of course, the one-piece front used by the racers. A tidy one-piece front will give new meaning to the term engine accessibility and really does look the part, too. Motobuild can supply one-piece front and rear ends (clips) as well as all the necessary fittings. In the USA Sports and Classics have a good range of one-piece fronts. As far as fasteners are concerned they are not just for one-piece fronts and you may wish to modify your bonnet to the lift-off type: this is quite straightforward and Motobuild can advise you on the best fittings to use. On the other hand you may simply wish to fit fasteners such as bonnet rubber fastenings or leather straps as a safety precaution.

Geoff Hale's racing Sprite, less the one-piece front he uses.

David Clarkson's supercharged Frogeye has the original one-piece front; if only they had all been designed to open this way! (courtesy David Clarkson)

vented that. What I can say,
though, is that should you come
across a car looking like a Ferrari
250GT but with Sprite running
gear it may just be you've
discovered a Speedwell Sprite.
Richard's own car not only has
the full body treatment, including a permanent hardtop, but
also has a Fiat 1500cc engine
fitted. Richard is compiling a
register of Speedwell Sprites and
will be pleased to hear from
owners of similarly modified
cars.

Conclusion
Finally, this has been a fairly

*Richard Rook's impressively
bodied Speedwell Sprite - I
would like to see MWS 5.5 inch
wire wheels and 175/70 tyres on
the car to really finish it off.*

short chapter given the fact
that a car is essentially made up
of a body and bits that fit onto
it! It remains to be said, though,
that before even beginning
modifications your car must be
structurally sound. If it's not
sound and is corroded then any
amount of body mods will not
make it any stronger and safety
must always come before
speed.
A final point is that help is at

hand as BL Heritage have now
started production of brand
new bodyshells for the Sprite/
Midget at a very reasonable
price. However, Heritage shells
are not available for cars with a
chassis number prefixed earlier
than GAN 4 or HAN 9 although,
as this book went to press,
Classic Automobiles of Rutland,
England, announced the availability of new Frogeye shells
which they have adapted from
the Heritage unit.

18 BASIC COMPETITION PREPARATION

Introduction

It is not possible for this chapter to give totally comprehensive instructions for race preparing your Sprite/Midget because regulations vary not only for different types of motorsport, but also for different series. The regulations you will need to refer to will be found in the current issue of the *RAC Blue Book* (UK) and the restrictions applying to the class of racing you will be entering or will be available from the sport's governing body in your country.

What this chapter will do is to point you in the right direction with regard to basic preparation and modifications which are generally mandatory in all classes for competing with a Sprite/Midget.

You may not even wish to compete in motorsports but rather intend to upgrade certain aspects of your car to make it safer in the event of an accident: for instance, fitting a roll bar or full harness. Since the seat of the car is where you are likely to spend most of your time this is a good place to start the chapter in earnest.

Competition seats

For competition use you will almost certainly wish to change your car's seats and for this reason the seat swop section

has been placed here. Alternatively, you may simply prefer different seats than the standard items. Whatever your reason for wanting to change your car's seats the options are many and varied.

The easy option, and possibly the cheapest way to upgrade the seating in your car, is to get seats from a later car with headrests: assuming you have the early type seats. The headrest will help prevent a whiplash injury to the neck in the event of an accident. Swopping from early to late seats is very simple and a workshop manual will give you all the advice you will need.

If you are fitting a sports or racing seat the main thing to consider is whether or not you will be using it in conjunction with a full race harness. If you are, be sure to choose a seat with harness slots. There is a wide selection of sports seats and these can be purchased by mail order from the manufacturer or a local tuning parts shop. Be sure to check the seat measurements before purchase, though.

A wide range of competition seats are available, but not all fit easily into the Sprite/Midget and in some cases not at all. The main problem is the seat width. This can be further aggravated if a roll bar is fitted. Because of this I will limit my recommendations to two seats

The Corbeau Riva seat fitted to my Sprite; note proximity to roll bar.

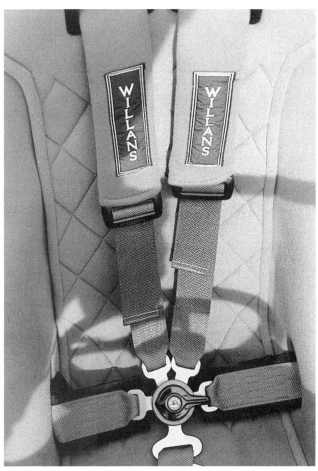

The Riva seat has the all important harness slots - used in my car for a Willans harness.

that I know will fit into the Sprite/ Midget which I have personally used.

The first I want to consider is the Corbeau GTA Clubman. This seat is somewhere between cheaper sports seats and the very expensive race seats which makes it a good choice and excellent value for money. It works well with a full harness and fits okay, albeit quite snugly.

A much better seat presently retailing at over three times the Clubman price, is the Riva competition seat also from Corbeau. The Riva is also available in more expensive versions in Kevlar and Carbon Fibre with Nomex trimming options. This is an amazing seat which fits extremely well in the car. The all important shoulder support area

of the seat is sufficiently narrower than other seats to clear the roll bar but it does fit very

The Riva seat fits tight against the door pillar as well as the roll bar.

tight to the B-post of the car. This seat is definitely my current number one choice for the Sprite/Midget, both because it fits well and is very comfortable. All sports and racing seats I know of either use a universal or a dedicated seat runner kit. I know the Corbeau fitting kits have excellent fitting instructions so I will not attempt to duplicate them here, but a couple of points are worth a mention. Firstly, it's possible to reduce the overall height of the installation by shortening some of the seat brackets without weakening the fitting. Alternatively, and depending on your own height ,you may have to fit the seat runners direct to the floor pan to allow enough head room to get in the car and this can be quite a tricky job. I found the best way to accomplish a direct fitting was to mark the floor out with a grid of masking tape and then biro mark bolt hole positions and crosscheck the installation before drilling the holes. A point to watch when drilling the seat holes and fitting the bolts is to be very careful not to drill

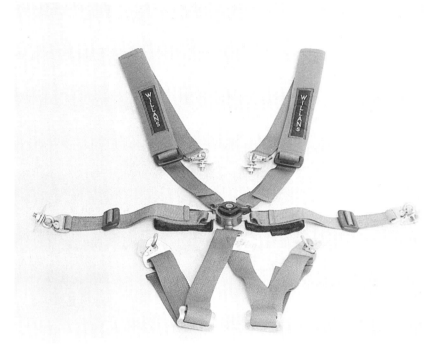

Willans 6-mounting point harness is superior to the 3-point harnesses I've used in the past.

through the petrol pipe and brake pipe which run along a rail underneath the floor pan!. Aside from that, fitting of the

Rear bulkhead mounting points are close together and it would be better if they could be spaced further apart to spread the load.

seat is quite straightforward. Corbeau also have a alloy subframe kit for the Riva which is lighter but not in-car adjustable for back and forward movement. I prefer the adjustable subframe as different people sometimes drive my car and this may be worth bearing in mind.

Old seat-belt anchor points can be used for some harness fittings.

The Willans mounting ring and reinforcing plate with belt clipped in.

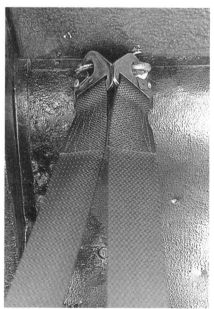

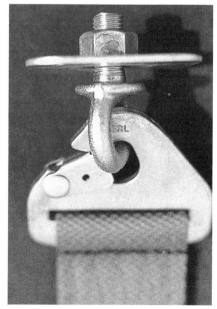

Full racing harness

Moving on from the seat an important consideration when it comes to competition preparation of your Sprite/Midget will be the racing harness. There is a wide choice of harnesses and these generally differ by the number of straps and fixing points. The greater number of fixing points the more the load is spread through the car. A greater number of straps also tends to produce more driver security. My own harness preference for competition is the Willans Club 6-point fixing, 6-strap harness. Willans have a sound reputation and I feel they can be trusted to produce a first class and safe product. I chose the 6 by 6 harness as I wanted maximum protection.

To fit a multi-point harness it's necessary to decide where the mounting points will be. On the Sprite/Midget these will invariably be on the floor and the rear bulkhead. A point to watch about the drilling of the mounts on the floor is to make sure you don't drill through the rigid brake line or rigid fuel line which will be very close to the ideal mounting points! Likewise, watch out for the rear fuel lines adjacent the fuel pump when drilling the rear bulkhead for the rear mounting points!. All of these areas should be sufficiently strong to be load bearing, assuming your car is structurally sound, in the event of an accident, but you may wish to weld in small reinforcing plates for extra security. Make sure you follow the manufacturer's instructions, in particular with regard to positioning the eye bolts & also care and use of the harness.

Once you have fitted the mounting points it only remains for you to clip in the harness. The beauty of the system is that should you ever decide to sell the car the harness can be unclipped, leaving the inexpensive mounting points behind.

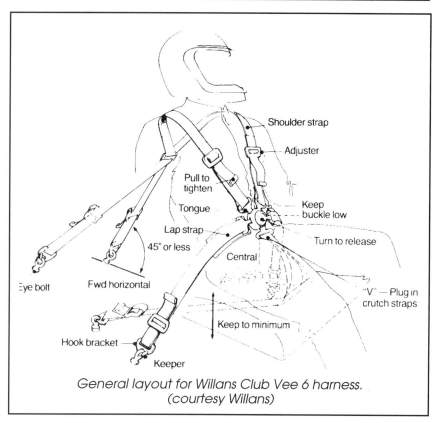

General layout for Willans Club Vee 6 harness.
(courtesy Willans)

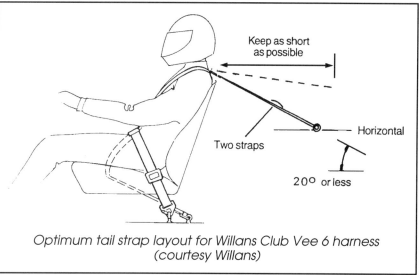

Optimum tail strap layout for Willans Club Vee 6 harness
(courtesy Willans)

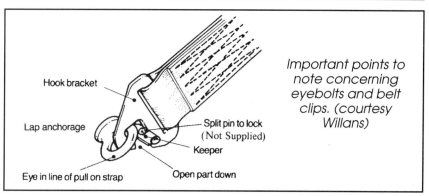

Important points to note concerning eyebolts and belt clips. (courtesy Willans)

Battery master isolator switch

Another standard safety requirement for most types of motorsport and race preparation is the fitting of a battery master isolator switch. Before fitting it is important to choose the right switch for your car. The principle difference, irrespective of make, is that there is one switch for dynamo-equipped cars and a different switch with alternator diode protection for alternator-equipped cars. Having purchased the appropriate switch for your car it is relatively straightforward to fit it. I consider the best site for the switch is on the top edge of the front wing (fender) in the corner, adjacent the scuttle panel (assuming you have retained the battery in the standard position). This switch location will not obscure your view and does not require any wiring to pass through the bulkhead. However, should you have a one-piece front then mounting the switch in the bulkhead is probably the best place.

To fit the switch drill the holes and bolt the switch in. Wiring the switch will require the removal of the battery live lead. Two new leads (heavy duty battery type) are then substituted and these can be made up by yourself or an auto electrical specialist. One lead runs from the battery live terminal to the switch and the other runs from the switch to the main battery feed point (usually the solenoid).

If you have the switch for alternator-equipped cars you will need to do some extra wiring to ensure the alternator is protected. To keep the leads tidy I suggest the use of P-clips or large wiring clips. A point to note is that I recommend fitting the leads to the battery last as this will eliminate the possibility of creating a dead short between a spanner, live wire and

Here is the unobtrusive battery master socket bolted onto the wing of my car.

the car body. You should also check that the switch leads do not foul the body once fitted. If

you can get hold of suitably sized connection covering boots I strongly recommend you use them: solenoid type rubber boots fit.

Flameproof bulkheads

It is more than likely that you will need to ensure all the bulkheads on your car are flameproof for any form of motorsport. I will cover the areas that you will need to concentrate on. The first, and main, area that needs sorting is the cardboard rear divider between the boot (trunk) and area at the back of the seats. Removing the cardboard is easy as it is only held in by screws: try and remove it in one piece so it can be used to make a template for its replacement which is best made in aluminium or steel. It can be

Left: Carpet and trim removal will reveal rear inner wing (fender) access apertures which should be plated over for competition.

Opposite page, left: Heating ducting to car neatly blocked off on Geoff Hale's Sprite. Note also hose from old heater outlet which bypasses heater matrix.

Opposite page, right: Lifeline plumbed-in fire extinguisher on Simon Page's car.

difficult to fabricate yourself without special tools and therefore I suggest that a local body shop do the job for you at minimal expense. Fixing can be by self-tapping screws or pop rivets but, remember, there should be no gaps.

Occasionally overlooked in race preparation are the cardboard side pieces that seal the rear inner wing (fender) from the boot area. These should also be replaced by light gauge sheet steel or aluminium as either a single plate or as three separate plates. The passenger side is easy to fit, again, using self-tapping screws or pop rivets. The driver's side is more difficult as the wiring loom for all the rear lights will need to pass through the lower panel. I drilled a large hole in this panel and, using a grommet, threaded the loom through it from the back. You will find that this can be a

little tricky and you might thread the loom from the front if easier in your car.

Peculiar to the Sprite/Midget is the blanking off of the heater air outlet from inside the engine bay and a suitable plate can be made once more in light gauge steel or aluminium sheet. Once fitted you will, of course, be unable to use the heater.

Fire extinguisher

You may already have a fire extinguisher in your car but, if you haven't, or even if you have, there are special considerations for motorsports. Lifeline is a top company for motorsports fire extinguishers and their products are even used by Williams Grand Prix Engineering in their F1 cars. They can supply you with a fully plumbed-in system which

means that the reservoir is in the car but the nozzle is under the bonnet adjacent to the carburettor(s). Triggering can be either automatic by a T-handled pull cable or electric switching. If your budget will stretch to it, the large cylinders can also be made in carbon fibre.

For my own car I chose a simple 5.5lb (2.5kg) hand-held unit with mounting bracket. Fitting is quite simple and there are only a couple of points to consider when choosing the mounting point. Keeping the centre of gravity low will mean a floor mounting which has the added benefit of reducing any possibility of the cylinder breaking loose in the event of an accident. Ease of access for the driver or passenger in an emergency is also something to consider and, finally, the unit needs to go where it will get

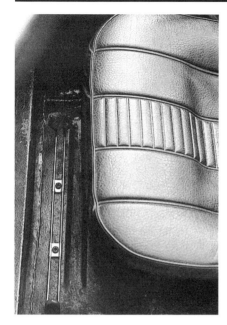

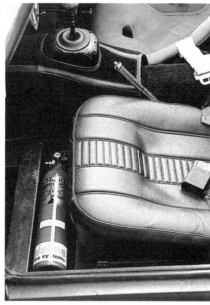

Far left: Fire extinguisher bracket sits neatly in front of passenger seat.

Left: The fire extinguisher in its bracket in my car.

it is definitely a job made easier with the car supported on axle stands. Not only does this make tightening bolts easier, it also eliminates any chance of drilling through the tyres: that may sound a bit patronising but I know a garage that once drilled through the spare tyre of a car when fitting the licence plate!

Should you wish them to, Safety Devices can fit your roll bar for you. Fitting times are in the region of an hour for the simpler non-FIA cages and about half a day for welded-in plates and FIA cages.

neither too hot or too cold. I chose a floor mounting on the passenger side of the car where it is unobtrusive yet ideally placed in an emergency. Fitting involves drilling a couple of holes. Being a right-hand drive car there was no danger of drilling through any brake or petrol lines but take car to note the position of the exhaust pipe.

Laminated windscreen

It is a competition requirement that the car has a laminated windscreen fitted instead of the normal toughened screen which crazes when it breaks. Fitting a screen to the Sprite/ Midget is much more involved than your average car and not a job easily done yourself, even with experience of windscreen fitting on other cars. Help is at hand, though, as Peter May Engineering provides an ex-change fitting service; however, any competent windscreen specialist should be able to cope.

Roll bar

I have used an Aley Aerody-namic roll bar in my Sprite and

then upgraded to fitting a FIA race approved bar with the removable diagonal brace with no problems whatsoever. There is a large choice of roll bars for the Sprite/Midget and since Safety Devices bought out Aley Bars some years ago, they are now all retailed under one roof in the UK.

Which type of bar you purchase will depend on the usage you intend to put the car to. The road use types can be simply bolted in yourself but the FIA approved rear bars need welded plates when fitted to make them race legal. I have fitted both bars myself and found the job quite straightfor-ward if the instructions supplied with the roll bar are followed. The only pointer I will give is that

Shell preparation

I have not mentioned shell preparation until now but it's a good idea to strengthen the shell by welding the seams. It may be that you even have a brand new Heritage shell to race prepare and if this is the case then Safety Devices can

Two different types of roll-over bar, both of which offer similar strength. The diagonal brace of the right-hand roll-over bar is removable for non-motorsport use.

Typical roll-over bar floor mounting.
(courtesy Aleybars)

completely race prep it to order. For instance, they can weld in the roll cage and flare the arches as well as seam welding the body for extra strength. All of the work that can be done on a new shell can also be done on an old shell, but is made much more difficult by the necessity to remove sealer, underseal, old paint, trim, etc.

Conclusion

That completes the race preparation chapter. Even if you are not going racing or rallying I hope that you will find it useful and that it makes your car more comfortable and a lot safer.

19 TUNING & DEVELOPMENT BY DYNOMOMETER

Introduction

Dynomometer tuning and development is about getting value for money from the engine in your car or maybe the engine you plan to put in your car. There are two distinct types of dynomometer: the engine dyno, and the chassis dyno. The first is a an engine test bed dyno where the engine is run independently of the car with power readings taken direct from the flywheel. The second, and more common, type is where the engine is in the car and the power readings are taken from the rear wheels via a pair of rollers. Because chassis dynos runs are taken from rollers this type of dyno is often known as the "rollers" or "rolling road" type dyno. For simplicity I will only cover the chassis dyno as it by far the most common.

What the dyno can do

The dyno is the best place to discover certain things about your engine: you will discover both real brake horsepower and torque output figures. You can also calibrate your speedometer and tachometer (rev counter). At the same time you can learn what exhaust emissions your engine is producing. Primarily, though, you will be running your car on the dyno to tune your engine for maximum

horsepower or simply to obtain the correct calibration for your carburettor and the optimum ignition setting. A point to note is that power figures obtained are at the rear wheels and cannot readily be converted to a flywheel figure. The other thing about the horsepower figure is that neither can it readily be compared to power figures other people achieve on other dynos. Finally, even consistent use of the same dyno can produce variations in horsepower figures. Therefore, the dyno should not be used to produce a set of figures to boast about at the paddock or bar, but rather more as an instrument to get the best result from your engine on the day you do your dyno runs.

A chassis dyno session

The first thing to do before a dyno run is choose which of the many dyno operators to go to. This choice may well be limited by geography but, whatever your choice, try and use the same dyno for future tests. Make sure the dyno operator is familiar with both the Sprite/Midget and whatever type of carburettor you are running on your engine. Further check that they have a suitable stock of needles or jets for that same carb. A point to remember is that the dyno is often only as

Peter Baldwin (left) discusses the engine specification of the author's car with him.

good as its operator and a poor technician will often only get a poor result. I have used the dyno at Marshall of Cambridge for some years now and can personally vouch for the expertise of Peter Baldwin who operates it. He is very familiar with the A-series engine as well as both SU and Weber carbs. He is also experienced with just about any other car or engine you can mention.

On all my dyno runs with Peter, I have always come away with more horsepower than I arrived with and also a smoother running engine. I know that a lot of his clientele are serious club racers who have themselves achieved good results on the track and some are Sprite/Midget racers.

When I do a dyno run I always take a notepad and pen (and hopefully someone to take notes) to keep a record of what is learnt in the session and for future reference. I also take a note of what my current ignition timing and carburettor calibration settings are for use in the session and to note changes. Before I even begin my dyno runs I always have a chat to Peter about what changes I have made to my engine and ignition and carburettor. I will also discuss any problems

As well as providing information on engine horsepower and torque output, the dyno can be used to calibrate speedometers, too. Here, my car's doing a genuine stationary 86/87mph.

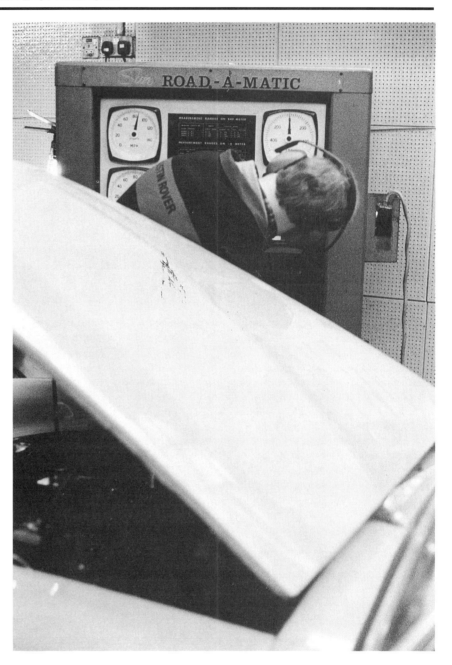

experienced with the engine and what I am hoping to achieve from the session. This helps Peter know what to look for and how to best spend the time. From then on I follow Peter's instructions.

The first job is to drive the car onto the rollers and get the wheels nice and central. Peter will chock the front wheels and proceed to attach his instruments which will include an exhaust gas analyser and wires to the ignition system.

I'll jump into the car and start the engine ready for the first part of the session which will be a run in neutral just to check the ignition system is working okay. If, for instance, the engine had a bad lead or arcing distributor cap it would show up on the tuning equipment. The first rolling run is usually done at a low engine speed simply to establish a good ignition setting. Peter does this by swinging the distributor while you are driving the car. The engine speed should be equal to the maximum advance the distributor will produce which will be around the middle power range of the engine. This is followed by a static check where Peter is now able to tell you what the static setting will be, (*ie* 8 degrees TDC, etc.). The figure will be unique to your engine and set-up and is the figure to note for future reference. If you are using a non-standard distributor it is helpful if you can tell Peter whose make and what model it is, such as "Microdynamics Rally", etc., before you do these checks. If you are really serious about ignition it is possible to take optimum readings up the rev range and plot them. This information can then be used

for a distributor re-curve to the ideal curve for your car's engine. My Microdynamics distributor has always been very close to ideal but after a previous session I had some slight changes made and, subsequently, these were verified as an improvement.

Following on from the slow engine speed run the next one will see how the engine performs up through the power range and the operator (in my case Peter) will be watching the CO gas analysis to see if the

mixture is too rich or too weak at any point in the rev range. It is important for the operator to know to what use the car's engine is likely to be put to as this will affect the final mixture strength settings. My car's engine has always run close to a full race mixture strength at full throttle, even though the car is only used on the road. Once the carburation settings are correct then a full power run can be taken which will give you the set of numbers you have been looking for. You may

Their dyno may not be as new as other operator's but Peter's vast knowledge and experience still makes Marshall's my number one choice.

even wish to take power readings at 500rpm increments to plot a power curve for your own use. Whatever you decide, I have found that the more information you can discover about your engine the better. Whilst you have been doing all your dyno runs, hopefully you will have kept a close eye on water and oil temperatures. Cars can run hotter than usual on the dyno, despite the presence of a large fan in the dyno bay to cool your engine in the absence of the normal airflow you would expect if the car was being driven on the road. But if you have any sort of cooling inadequacy this is when you will discover it.

When you have finished all your dyno runs quite often the operator will invite you to drive your car up the road for a short

test to ascertain if everything feels okay. This is quite an experience as the car will nearly always not only feel a lot smoother but should also be more powerful. Whilst completing this part of the test be mindful both of the noise your car generates and the local

speed limits.

Once everything is complete then it is time to pay the bill for the time spent on the dyno, which is usually an hourly rate plus the cost of jets and/or needles. The price is usually fairly modest ,given the gains in horsepower you will have made and the data you will have hopefully learnt from the session and the operator.

This chapter is entitled development as well as dyno tuning and any development of your car's engine should always be followed by a visit to the dyno. Where finances prohibit this for any length of time then you should keep a record of what changes have been made and what affects they had. This will serve both as a guide and record which will be useful for future reference but can never be a substitute for dyno runs. Finally, write up your dyno notes when you get back home as they will serve as a useful reference which may be invaluable in the future.

20 PROFILES OF COMPETITION SPRITES & MIDGETS

Introduction

Although the main thrust of this book is aimed at the reader who wishes to modify a road car, I feel sure even the most hardened racer will learn at least one useful fact on reading the book, if not many, many more. However, it's also interesting for a reader modifying his standard road car to be aware of the other end of the spec-trum and learn what it is possible to do with a racing Sprite/ Midget. For this short section I have looked at a couple of racing cars and a rally car that have achieved a good measure of competition success.

Turbocharged Frogeye Sprite

Cars don't come much more unusual or, indeed, modified than Simon Page's racing Frogeye Sprite. When I first spoke to Simon on the 'phone there were two items on his car that held particular interest for me. The first was that he had fitted the Toyota 5-speed gearbox conversion, which you can

The very successful Motobuild Midget. Driver Robb Gravett went on to achieve a lot of success with a Ford Sierra, and I believe the Midget went to Japan.
(courtesy Michael C.Brown)

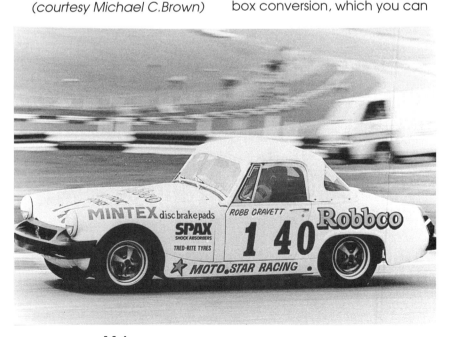

Karl Barras' race car in the paddock at Silverstone. Note full roll cage and exhaust exit point.

read about in the gearbox chapter, and the second was that he runs a turbocharged engine. Although David Vizard covers A-series engine turbocharging in *Tuning BL's A-series Engine* , I was interested in Simon's car because, initially, he used the Metro Turbo system

'off the shelf' although, at a later stage, he adapted the conversion to include a modified Montego intercooler. An additional point of interest in the intercooler fitting is that he uses temperature stickers to monitor effective temperatures which is an idea I had previously only seen used on braking systems. I was not surprised to hear of a turbocharged Sprite but was initially surprised to find that not many people have taken this

route. Having seen Simon's car, however, I can now better appreciate the complexity of the system but believe that this kind of modification is well within the realms of readers' road cars.

Looking at Simon's installation it can be seen that it is a good deal more sophisticated than

Simon Page well ahead in his turbocharged Frogeye (Bugeye) Sprite.

the standard Metro System and it was interesting to see Microdynamics electronics systems being put to good use. The turbo installation obviates the need for an LCB-type manifold and the pipe from the turbo housing runs through a silencer to a short and tidy pipe which exits the side of the car well clear from any kerbs, unlike normally aspirated side exhaust cars. The turbo system also requires a non-standard fuel system which uses twin pumps, one at each end of the car, one low pressure and one high. The Toyota gearbox is much stronger for the job of handling

Above: The power plant of Simon Page's Frogeye Sprite.

Right: A closer look at the turbo installation on Simon's Frogeye.

Fabricated rear suspension and Ford Anglia back axle in Simon's much modified Frogeye.

the power output of the turbocharged engine in both power and, particularly, torque. The power is fed through an AP single plate sintered race clutch. The Toyota conversion bellhousing was relieved to accommodate this latter item. It isn't just the engine and transmission that are unusual on this car. Both the front and rear suspension are very well developed. Of particular interest was the use of a Ford Anglia axle with Quaife diff. The axle installation is one of a pair that was proposed, designed and built by Simon and a friend - Chris

Norris. The axle uses Spax shock absorbers and a Watts linkage with anti-roll bar - all fully rose-jointed. The front suspension is a little more conventional with a modified Armstrong lever arm unit that has a second top suspension link.

The front stub axle mates to another Ford part, this time Cortina disc and calliper, but the discs are drilled. All the brake linings are Ferodo. I particularly liked the rose-jointed anti-roll bar link also on the front. The rest of the car is, of course, also modified for racing and I cannot finish this brief description of Simon's car without mentioning his trade-mark, a genuine number 8 Pool ball which has been drilled and tapped for use as a gearknob. All in all, this is a very interesting race car and I trust it will be an inspiration for owners of other race cars and road cars alike.

Racing Midget

Peter May's race car may be a lot less flamboyant than Simon's but nevertheless has several interesting features.

Being in the business of preparing race cars, engines and gearboxes is an advantage when running your own car and Peter's car was as neat as I expected it to be. Although running a conventionally tuned engine, the car has several interesting features worth mentioning.

On the rear suspension Peter has modified the Spax telescopic conversion so that the shock absorbers act in the vertical plane (which is how they were designed to act), a

conversion Peter can also sell to you. Peter also sells Panhard rod kits but on his own car he uses a specially fabricated item that is welded to the axle case rather than bolted. In the engine bay the car uses two engine steady/tie rods which are rose-jointed. These rods prevent excessive engine movement.

The car uses a large disc brake conversion but, in common with most racers, does not use a servo. The body is very tidy and I particularly liked the cut-out and ducting to direct air onto the front brakes. I really liked this

One of the two engine steady bars on Peter May's car.

Below: Peter May's race car in the paddock at Silverstone. Note carefully crafted NACA-type duct in door and air outlet at the rear of the front wing.

Above: Phil Bollen's 1967 Mk 3 Midget which is used to compete in historic rallying.

Above centre and right: Homemade, but nevertheless effective, sump guard fitted to Phil Bollen's rallying Midget. When fitting this type of guard, make sure the design allows adequate airflow through the engine bay.

car and it is one of the tidiest racing Midgets I have come across.

Rally Midget

The last car to feature in this chapter is Phil Bollen's rally Midget. This is a fairly standard car due to the class of rallying Phil competes in.

The engine modifications include K&N air filters, LCB manifold and RC40 exhaust silencer, alternator conversion and an oil cooler. Phil's car also has racing seats, harnesses, a battery master isolator switch and a sump guard. The rest of the car is pretty much standard.

The reason that I particularly wanted to feature this car is to illustrate that you don't need pots of money and enormous technical expertise to have a

lot of fun with your car ,whether you enter it for competition or not, just lots of enthusiasm.

Pete Holden racing in his Ron Hopkinson sponsored Midget: does he really slow down for horses? (courtesy Philip Rogers)

21 INSURANCE

Introduction

Just in case you hadn't realised, it *is* necessary to tell your insurance company about the modifications you make to your car. However, not all modifications will result in a loading of the premium though, of course, large increases in power invariably will. My own modified car has been insured, modifications and power declared, for many years and the car's insurance still represents good value for money.

Notes on insurance

I spoke to Austin Healey insurance expert Alan Ling of T F Bell & Co., a company of insurance brokers, to ask why insurance for the modified Sprite and Midget was so reasonable and also to ask what type of modifications caused the greatest premium loading.

Because even a modified Sprite or Midget is still a classic car and unlikely to be as recklessly abused as modern performance cars, particularly 'hot hatches', they represent a better insurance risk and, therefore, premiums are lower. However, the broker and underwriter will ask what kind of use the car is going to be put and unusual uses may well attract surcharges because normal cover excludes motorsports, competitions etc.

Suspension and braking modifications will not usually increase insurance (converting an early drum/drum car to disc/drum is an example), but an increase in power will almost certainly lead to a loading, for example, of 10% premium for 10% more power. An increase in engine power with no attendant braking, suspension or safety modifications will be viewed unfavourably by the underwriter. It's also possible that the underwriter will ask to have an independent engineer certify that the car is safe and roadworthy if it is extensively modified or modified in an unusual way. An important aspect of insurance is that, having spent money on restoring the car and then a sizeable sum on modifications, you don't want to see it stolen, crashed or written off only to be compensated at a value equal to a standard car. You should be able to find an insurer who will accept an agreed value for your car, even if modified, but you may have to accept an annual mileage restriction in return.

Finally, I know that Alan Ling and T F Bell & Co. are only too happy to advise on insurance and you may wish to give them a call *before* embarking on really ambitious modifications. Failure to notify your insurance company of modifications can, of course, not only render your insurance invalid but is also a

MODIFIED VEHICLE REPORT (Excluding Kit Cars)

Name _____   Policy Number _____

IMPORTANT: PLEASE ANSWER ALL THE FOLLOWING QUESTIONS PRECISELY giving full details of any modification to the Maker's specification of your vehicle. If, on receipt of this form, further information is required THE COMPANY RESERVES THE RIGHT TO HAVE THE VEHICLE INSPECTED BY AN ENGINEER OF ITS OWN CHOICE BUT WILL NOT BE RESPONSIBLE FOR ANY FEE CHARGED IN CONNECTION WITH SUCH INSPECTION.

1.

Make and Model of Vehicle	Type of Body e.g. Saloon, Coupe etc.	Registration Mark	C.C./H.P.	Year of Make	Value	Date of Expiry of current D.O.E. Test Certificate

Engine Number	Chassis Number	Body Colour	Mileometer Reading

2. ENGINE AND TRANSMISSION

Has any part of the engine and/or transmission been altered from the Manufacturer's standard specification for your vehicle? If "Yes" complete the following: Yes ☐ No ☐

(a) Make and Model (e.g. G.T. etc) of engine fitted _____

(b) Make, type and how many carburettors fitted _____

(c) Detail ALL modifications to engine. If none state 'NONE' _____

(d) Is gearbox and final drive ratio original? If 'NO' give details _____   Yes ☐ No ☐

3. SUSPENSION AND STEERING

Has any part of the suspension and/or steering mechanism been altered from the Manufacturer's standard specification for your vehicle. If 'YES' complete the following: Yes ☐ No ☐

(a) Detail ALL modifications to suspension (including shock absorbers) and/or suspension mounting points. If none state 'NONE'

(b) Detail ALL modifications to steering mechanism. If none state 'NONE' _____

NOTE:-Colour photographs (front, side and rear) will be required for any vehicle with raised/jacked-up rear suspension

4. BRAKES

(a) State type of brakes fitted to your vehicle:

POSITION	FRONT AXLE	REAR AXLE
TYPE OF BRAKES (tick as appropriate)	DISC ☐	DISC ☐
	DRUM ☐	DRUM ☐

(b) Is a servo unit fitted?   Yes ☐ No ☐

(c) Has any part of the braking system been altered from the Manufacturer's standard specification for your vehicle? If 'YES' detail all modifications and state the size of the brake discs/drums where these have been altered.   Yes ☐ No ☐

Continued over

5. BODY AND CHASSIS   Yes ☐ No ☐

(a) Have any body panels been replaced with Glass Reinforced Plastic/Fibre Glass? If 'YES' state:

(i) the panels which have been so replaced _____

(ii) details of any strengthening brackets and/or bars fitted _____

(b) Detail any other modification to the body or chassis (e.g. wheel arch extensions etc.). If none state 'NONE'

6. WHEELS   Yes ☐ No ☐

(a) Are wheel spacers fitted? If 'YES' state make and size _____   ☐ ☐

(b) Have different wheels from the Manufacturer's standard specification for your vehicle been fitted? If 'YES' complete the following: ☐ ☐

(i) state make, size and type

(ii) Are the wheels of the 'Split Rim/Banded Rim' variety? If 'YES' by whom were they made?   ☐ ☐

7. TYRES

Complete the following:

POSITION	FRONT NEARSIDE	FRONT OFFSIDE	REAR NEARSIDE	REAR OFFSIDE	SPARE
Type of Ply (tick as appropriate)	Radial ☐	Radial ☐	Radial ☐	Radial ☐	Radial ☐
	Cross ☐	Cross ☐	Cross ☐	Cross ☐	Cross ☐
	Size	Size	Size	Size	Size ....

8. ACCESSORIES

Please detail any extras and accessories (e.g. additional instrumentation, lighting, etc.) If none state 'NONE'

9. ADDITIONAL MODIFICATIONS

Please detail any other modifications or alterations to the vehicle. If none state 'NONE' _____

NOTE:- Colour photographs (front, side and rear) will be required for any vehicle which has been 'Customised'

10. (i) By whom were the modifications carried out? _____

(ii) State their qualifications _____

(iii) Date of modifications _____

I/We hereby declare that to the best of my/our knowledge and belief the statements and particulars above and overleaf are true and correct and that I/We have not withheld any material information whether the subject of a question or not. I/We understand that failure to disclose all facts known to me/us which would be considered by the insurer as likely to influence assessment or acceptance of the cover required could render the policy inoperative. (NOTE — Where there is any doubt about whether facts would be considered material those facts should be disclosed). I/We agree that the statements and particulars above and overleaf shall in conjunction with my/our original proposal form the basis of the contract between me/us and the insurer.

Date _____   Signed _____

You should keep a record (including copies of letters) of all information supplied to us for the purpose of entering into this insurance. A copy of this form will be supplied by us on request within three months of completion.

An example of the kind of questionaire you are likely to be asked to fill in when you request insurance for a modified car. (courtesy T. F. Bell & Co.)

civil offence (in the UK, at least)

Readers should be aware that various special policies are available for the Sprite and Midget, often through the owners' clubs and registers.

22 APPENDIX

Introduction

Here is a list of useful suppliers, those who supply services and clubs which should help you to track down the parts and services you require. Some of these companies are well known, other less so, but in many cases I have had first hand dealings and am happy to recommend them.

Specialists & Suppliers (International)

Abingdon Motors
192 Annerly Road
BRISBANE
Australia

Advanced Products (K&N air filters)
Wilderspool Causeway
WARRINGTON
Cheshire WA4 6QP
England
Tel: 0925 36950

AP Racing
Wheler Road
Seven Stars Industrial Estate
COVENTRY CV3 4LB
England
Tel: 0203 639595

AP Automotive Products
Brakes Division
Tachbrook Road
LEAMINGTON SPA
Warwickshire CV31 3ER
England
Tel: 0926 470000

Automotive Components Ltd (Compomotive Wheels)
No 4 - 6 Wulfrun Industrial Estate
Stafford Road
WOLVERHAMPTON
West Midlands WV10 6HG
England

T. F. Bell & Co (Insurance Brokers) Ltd
39 Station Road
HINCKLEY
Leicestershire LE10 1AP
England
Tel: 0455 251199

Brembo Discs - *see* Contract Distribution Services Ltd

British Motor Industry Heritage Trust
Castle Road
STUDLEY
Warwickshire B80 7AJ
England
Tel: 052785 4014

British Wire Wheel
1600 Mansfield Street
SANTA CRUZ
USA

Carcraft
Motor Engineers & Restorers
Nacton Road Industrial Estate
IPSWICH
Suffolk IP3 ORR
England
Tel: 0473 723991

Classic Automobiles of Rutland
MELTON MOWBRAY
England
Tel: 0664 65936

Contract Distribution Services Ltd (Brembo Discs)
Unit 7
Red Sands Road
KIDDERMINSTER
Worcestershire DY10 2LQ
England
Tel: 0562 67881

Corbeau Seats (Protech Seating Ltd)
Ivyhouse Industrial Area
HASTINGS
East Sussex
England
Tel: 0424 435480

Cosmos Trading Co. Inc
20-7 Nihonbasi Kodenmacho
TOKYO
Japan

Dellow Automotive
37 Daisy St
Revesby
SYDNEY
Australia2212
Tel: 0101 2 774 4419

Facet Enterprises Inc

Automotive Components
Marketing
ELMIRA
NY 14903
USA
Tel: 0101 607 737 8243

Fuel System Enterprises Ltd
180 Hersham Road
HERSHAM
Walton on Thames
Surrey KT12 5QE
England
Tel: 0932-231973

GMA Sas (for MWS wheels)
Di Gallorni Marco
27100 PAVIA
Italy

Goodridge (UK) Ltd
Exeter Airport Business Park
EXETER
Devon EX5 2UP
England
Tel: 0392 69090

Hardy Engineering - Gearboxes
268 Kingston Road
LEATHERHEAD
Surrey
England
Tel: 0372 378927

Hobbs Sport Ltd (Goodridge
Hose)
Unit 4D
Brentmill Industrial Estate
SOUTH BRENT
Devon TQ10 9YT
England
Tel: 0364 73956

Induction Technology Group
Ltd
Unit 5
Fairfield Court
Seven Stars Industrial Estate
Whitley
COVENTRY
West Midlands CV3 4LJ
England
Tel: 0203 305386

Janspeed Engineering Ltd
Castle Road
SALISBURY
Wiltshire SP1 3SQ
England
Tel: 0722 321833

Kool Louvres
14 Walton Way
AYLESBURY
Buckinghamshire HP21 7JL
England
Tel: 0296 88548

Lifeline Fire and Safety Ltd
Lifeline House
Daish Way
NEWPORT
Isle of Wight PO30 5XJ
England
Tel: 0983 521921

Richard Longman & Co
5 Airfield Road
Airfield Way Industrial Estate
CHRISTCHURCH
DorsetBH23 3TG
England
Tel: 0202 486569

Long Motor Corporation - *see*
Victoria British Ltd

Marshall of Cambridge
Jesus Lane
CAMBRIDGE
Cambridgeshire CB5 8BH
England
Tel: 0223 62211

Peter May Eng. Ltd
92 Windmill Hill
HALESOWEN
West Midlands B63 2BY
England
Tel: 0384 635691

MG Parts Centre
c/o Bill Richards
5 Alden Terrace
HOWELL
New Jersey 07731
USA

Microdynamics
PO Box 51
CATERHAM
Surrey CR3 6UD
England
Tel: 0883 349281

Minor Mania Ltd
1/3 Hale Lane
Mill Hill Broadway
Mill Hill
LONDON NW7 3NU

England
Tel: 081 959 0818

Mini Spares Centre Ltd
29-31 Friern Barnet Road
LONDON N11 1NE
England
Tel: 081 368 6292

Moss Motors Ltd
7200 Hollister Avenue
PO Box 847
GOLETA
California 93116
USA
Tel: 805 968 1041

Moss Sprite & Midget B, C, V8
Centre,
22-28 Manor Road
RICHMOND
Surrey TW9 1YB,
England
Tel: 081 948 6665

Motobuild Ltd
328 Bath Road
HOUNSLOW
Middlesex TW4 7HW
England
Tel: 081 570 5342/081 572
5437

Motorsport Equipment
MISSISSAUGA
Ontario
Canada

Motor Wheel Service (MWS)
Southern Region
Langley Business Park
Station Road
LANGLEY
Berkshire SL3 6EP
England
Tel: 0753 49360

Motor Wheel Service (MWS)
Northern Region
Shentonfield Road
Sharston
Wythenshawe
MANCHESTER M22 4RW
England
Tel: 061 428 7773

MWS/Leberfinger
Kiebitzhorn 31
2000 HAMBOURG-
BARSBUTTEL

Germany

Northwest Import Parts
10915 S.W. 64th Avenue
PORTLAND
OR 97219
USA
Tel: 0101 503 245 3806

Octagon Spares BV
Mr G de Groot
Burg Van Niekerklaan 19
2182 GK HILLEGOM
Holland

Oselli Engineering
Ferry Hinksey Road
OXFORD
Oxfordshire OX2 OBY
England
Tel: 0865 248 100

Quaife Power Transmissions
R.T. Quaife Eng Ltd
Botany Industrial Estate
Sovereign Way
TONBRIDGE
Kent TN9 1RS
England
Tel: 0732 353747

Reco-Prop
Unit 4
Newtown Trading Estate
Chase Street
LUTON
Beds LU1 3QZ
England
Tel: 0582 412110

Ripspeed International
54 Upper Fore Street
Edmonton
LONDON N18 2SS
England
Tel: 081 803 4355

Richard E. Rooks (Speedwell
Sprites)
945 Alfred Street
BROOKFIELD
Wisconsin 53005
USA
Tel: 0101 414 784 5758

Ron Hopkinson MG Parts
Centre
850 London Road
DERBY
Derbyshire DE2 8WA

England
Tel:0332 756056

Safety Devices
176 Exning Road
NEWMARKET
Suffolk CB8 0AF
England
Tel:0638 681421

Schofield & Samson Ltd
Tuscany Wharf
4b Orsman Road
LONDON N1
England
Tel: 071 739 6817/8

Serck Marston (Competition
Products Division)
5-7 Cullen Way
Park Royal Road
LONDON NW10 6LY
England
Tel: 081 965 5442

Serck Marston
Heming Road
Washford Industrial Estate
REDDITCH
Worcestershire B98 0DZ
England
Tel: 0527 510111

Seven Enterprises Ltd
716 Bluecrab Road
NEWPORT NEWS
VA 23606
USA
Tel: 0101: 804 873 0007

Spax Ltd
Telford Road
BICESTER
Oxfordshire OX6 OUU
England
Tel: 0869 244771

Sports & Classics
512 Boston Post Road
DARIEN
Conn 06820
USA
Tel: 0101 (203) 655 8731

Stack Limited (Tachometer/
revcounter)
Wedgewood Road
BICESTER
Oxfordshire OX6 7UL
England

Tel: 0869 240404

Stockbridge Racing (Willans
Safety Harness)
Grosvenor Garage
STOCKBRIDGE
Hampshire
England
Tel: 0264 810712

Toyota Sport
Toyota (GB) Ltd
Technical Centre
8 Steer Place
Bonehurst Road
Salfords
REDHILL
Surrey RH1 5EF
England
Tel: 0293 774866

Victoria British Ltd
PO Box 14991
LENEXA
Kansas 66285-4991
USA
Tel: 0101 (913) 541 1525

Willans - *see* Stockbridge
Racing

Clubs & organizations

AUSTRALIA

Austin Healey

Austin Healey Club of New
South Wales
PO Box A471,
SYDNEY SOUTH
NSW 2000
Australia

Austin Healey Club of Queens-
land
A.Keepence
2 Dorricott Crescent
GOODNA
Queensland 4300
Australia

Austin Healey Club of South
Australia
PO Box 10
NORWOOD 5067
South Australia

Austin Healey Club of Victoria
PO Box 105
KEW
Victoria 3101
Australia

Austin Healey Club of Western
Australia
PO Box 70
MAYLANDS
WA 6051
Australia

Austin Healey Owners Club
Branch
Ed Janze
62 Wales Street
FOOTSCRAY
Victoria
Australia

Sprite Car Club Australia
P.Turley
2-11 Soldeirs Avenue
HARBOARD 939-1776
Australia

MG

MG Car Club,
Geelong Branch
c/o Terry Egan

4 Windmill Street
Newtown
GEELONG
Victoria 3220
Australia

MG Car Club Newcastle (Inc)
Mrs Fran Hodgson
PO Box 62A
NEWCASTLE
NSW 2300
Australia

MG Car Club of South Aus-
tralia
David pearson
72, Battams Road
MARDEN 5070
South Australia

MG Car Club of West Australia
GPO Box U1924
PERTH 6001
Western Australia

MG Owners Club Western
Australia
Ric Leonhardt
PO Box 181
MOUNT LAWLEY
WA 6050
Australia

Townsville MG & CS Car Club
PO Box 1307
TOWNSVILLE
Queensland 4810
Australia

AUSTRIA

Austin Healey

Austin Healey Club of Austria
P.Novak
Plankenmaistrasse 14
1220 WIEN
Austria

MG

MG Club of Austria
Rudolph Entrich
Postfach 39
1071 WIEN
Austria

BELGIUM

Austin Healey

Austin Healey Club of Belgium
M.Aerts

Grand Moulin
Rue de Moulin 1
B-5900 JODOIGNE,
Belgium

MG
MG Club of Belgium
Henri Simar
Rue de College
BP 172
B-4800 VERVIERS
Belgium

CANADA
Austin Healey
Austin Healey Club of Southern
Ontario
I.Marr
82 Paradise Road
HAMILTON
Ontario L8S 3SB
Canada

Austin Healey Owners Assoc.
of British Columbia
PO Box 80274
BURNABY
British Columbia
Canada V5H 3X5

MG
Alberta MG Car Club
4704 32nd Avenue
CALGARY
Alberta T3E 0X5
Canada

Canadian Classic MG Club
6362 Chatham Street
WEST VANCOUVER
BC V7W 2E2
Canada

Edmonton MG T Club
Phil Lulman
RR2
NEW SAREPTA
Alta T0B 3MO
Canada

MG Car Club Toronto
John Peterson
PO Box 64
Station R
TORONTO
Ontario M4G 3Z3
Canada

Ontario MGA/MGB

PO Box 130
KINGSTON
Ontario V9B 1YL
Canada

Victoria MG Car Club
1201 Mildred Place
VICTORIA
BC V8Z 7A3
Canada

Windsor-Detroit MG Club
Frank Lucente
854 Hall Avenue
WINDSOR
Ontario N9A 2M3
Canada

DENMARK
Austin Healey
Austin Healey Club of Denmark
H.Binger
Klovereng 9
2950 VEDBAEK
Denmark

MG
MG Car Club Danish Centre
Andrew Jaconbsen
Drosselvej 5
3600 FREDERIKSSUND
Denmark

MG Club of Denmark
Post Box 1656
2720 VANLOSE
Denmark

FINLAND
MG Club of Finland
Tero Harkonen
Vanamontie 4 D 110,
01350 VANTAA
Finland

FRANCE
Austin Healey
Austin Healey Club of France
S.Bonello
Val Flory
9 Rue Alexandre Dumas
78160 MARLY LE ROY
France

MG
MG Club of France
49 Rue Marchal Joffre

ST AVERTIN 37170
France

GERMANY
Austin Healey
Austin Healey Club of Germany e.V.,
Torsten Franzen
Bodmanstrasse 12-14
8960 KEMPTEN
Germany

MG
Munster MG Owners Club
Allan Knight
Einenerstr. 26
4410 WARENDORF 3
Germany

GREAT BRITAIN
Austin Healey
Austin Healey Club of Great
Britain
Mrs C.Holmes
4 Saxby Street
LEICESTER
Leics LE2 0ND
England

Austin Healey Club (UK) Sprite
Register
Bob Kemp
The White House
34 Main Street
Overseal
BURTON ON TRENT
Staffs DE12 6LG
England
Tel:0283 760434

Sprite & Midget Club
63 Littledean
Yate
BRISTOL
Avon BS17 4UQ
England

MG
MG Car Club
Kimber House
PO Box 251
ABINGDON
Oxfordshire OX14 1FF
England
Tel:0235 555552

MG Owners Club
Freepost

SWAVESEY
Cambridgeshire CR4 1BR
England
Tel:0954 31125

HOLLAND
Austin Healey
Austin Healey Club of Holland
B.Schaap
Graskamp 3
4175 CX HAAFTEN
Holland

MG
MG Car Club Holland
Marianne de Vries
Voorstraat 97
3311 EM DORDRECHT
Holland

MG Norzd
E.T.Hofman
De Rung 3
9313 TE LEUTINGE
Holland

IRELAND
Austin Healey Club of Ireland
B.Byrne
11 Marley Close
Marley Grange
RATHFARNHAM
Dublin 16
Ireland

ISRAEL
Israel MG Owners Club
Mina (Mickie) Grinker
7 Habanim Street
RAMAT-HASHASON 47216
Israel

ITALY
Austin Healey
Scuderia Austin Healey Sprite
Italia
A & L Macchi
Via Vincenzo Foppa 6
20144 MILAN
Italy

MG
MG International Florence Cars
Federico Mattaliano
Via del Clasio nr 21
50135 FIRENZE

Italy

JAPAN

Austin Healey Club of Japan
Hiroshi Takemori
1542-17 Yabe Cho Totsuka Ku
YOKOHAMA CITY
244 Japan

LUXEMBOURG

MG Car Club of Luxembourg
Tom Maathius
1 Rue Tomm
9454 FOUHREN
Luxembourg

MALAYSIA

Auto Travellers Club
Wong Fook Keong
219A Jalan Mahkota
Taman Maluri
Cheras 55100 KUALA
LUMPUR
W.Malaysia

NEW ZEALAND

Austin Healey
Austin Healey Club of New
Zealand
PO Box 899
PAPAKURA
New Zealand

MG
MG Car Club (Wellington
Centre Inc)
M.Hellberg
PO Box 3135
WELLINGTON
New Zealand

NORWAY

Norsk MG Klubb
Bjoern Rygh & Wenche Sand
CA Pihlsgt 2
0273 OSLO 2
Norway

PORTUGAL

MG Club de Portugal
R.Pardall Monteiro
Lt 248-Loja-91
1900 LISBON
Portugal

SLOVENIA

Codelli Classic & Sportscar
Club
dr. Mirko Prosek
Goce Delceva 58,
YU-61000 LJUBLLJANA
Slovenia

SOUTH AFRICA

Austin Healey
Austin Healey Club of Southern
Africa
PO Box 33342
JEPPESTOWN 2043
South Africa

MG
Pietermatitzburg MG Owners
Club
PO Box 424
Hilton 3245
NATAL
South Africa

SPAIN

Costa Blanca Sports Car Club
Ann Perry
Burzon 3813
Camina Del Estret 93
Pinar del Abagat 48
03724 Moraira
ALICANTE
Spain

SWEDEN

Austin Healey
Austin Healey Club of Sweden
Gunnar Berger
Bandyvagen 35
126 62 HAGERSTEN
Sweden

MG
Goran Tordne
Haratjarnvagen 6
93030 URSVIKEN
Sweden

Bengt Sanden
Ankaregaten 10
S 59172
MOTALA
Sweden

SWITZERLAND

Austin Healey
Austin Healey Club of Switzer-
land
H.J.Zschaler
Rebweg 17
8108 DALLIKON
Switzerland

MG
Anthony Richardson
1891 VEROSSAZ VALAIS
Switzerland

USA

Austin Healey
Austin Healey Assoc. of
Southern California
PO Box 4822
RIVERSIDE
CA 92515
USA

Austin Healey Club of America
c/o Richard Neville
21 Allen Lane
IPSWICH
MA 01938
USA

Austin Healey Club of America
Mrs E.Anderson
603 N.Euclid
ARLINGTON HEIGHTS
IL 60004
USA

Austin Healey Club of Oregon
Ron Johnson
13944 NE Freemont Court
PORTLAND
Oregon
USA

Austin Healey Club Pacific
Centre
PO Box 6197
SAN JOSE
CA 95150
USA

Austin Healey Sprite of
Hershey
R.Moses
1421 E.Chocolate Avenue
HERSHEY
PA 17033
USA

Cascade Austin Healey Club
PO Box 39
Lynnwood
WASHINGTON
WA 98046
USA

Sprite & Midgets Owners
Group
10135 Parrish View Drive
GILROY
CA 95030
USA

MG
American MG Assoc.
Frank Ochal
PO Box 11401
CHICAGO
IL 60611-0401
USA

Central Jersey MG Club
14 Birchwood Road
DENVILLE.
NJ 03031
USA

MG Car Club Central Jersey
Centre
Gregg Coogan
PO Box 435
CONVENT STATION
NY 07961
USA

MG Car Club Northwest
Central
Kevin Cobley
5204 NE 193rd Place
SEATTLE
Washington 98155
USA

MG Club
Steve Harding
1913D Darby Road
HAVERTOWN
PA 19083
USA

MG Club of Central Florida
Curtis Koom
309 E.Alpine Street
ALTAMONTE SPRINGS
Florida 32701
USA

MG Car Club DC Centre